SYMBOL AND POLITICS IN COMMUNAL IDEOLOGY
Cases and Questions

SYMBOL, MYTH, AND RITUAL SERIES

General Editor: Victor Turner

---

* Also available as a Cornell Paperback.

SYMBOL AND POLITICS IN COMMUNAL IDEOLOGY

Cases and Questions

Edited by SALLY FALK MOORE
and BARBARA G. MYERHOFF

Cornell University Press
ITHACA AND LONDON

First published 1975 by Cornell University Press.
Published in the United Kingdom by Cornell University Press Ltd., 2-4 Brook Street, London W1Y 1AA.

First printing, Cornell Paperbacks, 1975

International Standard Book Number (cloth) 0-8014-0988-8
International Standard Book Number (paperback) 0-8014-9157-6
Library of Congress Catalog Card Number 75-16810
Printed in the United States of America by York Composition Co., Inc.

Foreword

Recently both the research and theoretical concerns of many anthropologists have once again been directed toward the role of symbols—religious, mythic, aesthetic, political, and even economic—in social and cultural processes. Whether this revival is a belated response to developments in other disciplines (psychology, theology, philosophy, linguistics, to name only a few), or whether it reflects a return to a central concern after a period of neglect, is difficult to say. In recent field studies, anthropologists have been collecting myths and rituals in the context of social action, and improvements in anthropological field technique have produced data that are richer and more refined than heretofore; these new data have probably challenged theoreticians to provide more adequate explanatory frames. Whatever may have been the causes, there is no denying a renewed curiosity about the nature of the connections between culture, cognition, and perception, as these connections are revealed in symbolic forms.

Although excellent individual monographs and articles in symbolic anthropology or comparative symbology have recently appeared, a common focus or forum that can be provided by a topically organized series of books has not been available. The present series is intended to fill this lacuna. It is designed to include not only field monographs and theoretical and comparative studies by anthropologists, but also work by scholars in other disciplines, both scientific and humanistic. The appearance of studies in such a forum encourages emulation, and emulation can produce fruitful new theories. It is therefore our hope that the series will serve as a house of many mansions, providing hospitality for the practitioners of any discipline that has a serious and creative concern with comparative symbology. Too often, disciplines are sealed off, in sterile pedantry, from significant intellectual influences. Nevertheless, our primary aim is to bring to public attention works on ritual and myth written by anthropologists, and our readers will find a variety of strictly anthropological approaches ranging from formal analyses of systems of symbols to empathetic accounts of divinatory and initiatory rituals.

Symbol and Politics in Communal Ideology deals with the pursuit of communal harmony in planned, nonplanned, and antiplanned communities and fruitfully applies the extended-case method in linking "particular cases and situations to larger social contexts, to larger theoretical problems." The editors and contributors have quite clearly been influenced by the Manchester School of British social anthropology, so it is appropriate that the book should be dedicated to Max Gluckman, the founder and mainspring of the school. But the thrust of the book is not so much upon processes of conflict and conflict-resolution in communities—processes that occupy a central position in many Manchester monographs—as it is upon the relationship between what Sally Falk Moore, in her Epilogue, calls "processes of regularization, processes of situational adjustment, and the factor of indeterminacy."

Processes of regularization, Moore says, "produce conscious models, rules, organizations, customs, symbols, rituals, and categories, and seek to make them durable." Processes of situational adjustment are those "by means of which people . . . use whatever areas there are of inconsistency, contradiction, conflict, ambiguity, or open areas that are normatively indeterminate to achieve immediate situational ends." "Indeterminacy," for Moore, characterizes "the underlying quality of social life." She argues persuasively that "even within the social and cultural order there is a pervasive quality of partial indeterminacy. . . . Apparent determinacy, in the guise of regularities of classification, symbol, and of form, may veil fundamental instabilities and changes of content."

This uneasy apprehension of chaos informs Moore's thinking about the systematic schemata that members of would-be perduring groups devise to give order to their lives. The most harmonious-seeming ideologies, cosmologies, ritual systems, legal codes, and political constitutions have the chaos dragon in their hidden hearts. Such apparent pessimism masks a deep recognition of human freedom, and is a useful corrective to those theoretical positions that would subject all human action to the requirements of cognitively derived and tinctured "systems" and "programs" to which feeling and willing are ancillary. Moore, however, does not propose to substitute indeterminacy for regularity. She argues that the ever-changing relationship between social life and its cultural representation can be better understood if we take fully into account the processual quality of both: maintaining form is a process, manipulating formal rules is a process, undermining prestigious structures of authority is a process, and societies and cultures are fields of interpenetrating processes. Individual and group, communitas and legally structured systems of status roles, forces of systemic maintenance and forces of change, all are dependent on one another; their relationship is dialectical not polar.

The dynamic frame of reference of Moore and Barbara Myerhoff accounts for many of the crucial properties of ritual, mythic, and ideological symbols: their multivocality, complexity of associational linkages, ambiguity, open-endedness, primacy of feeling and willing over thinking, and their propensity to ramify into further semantic systems. Symbols are seen as triggers of social action, and of personal action in public arenas. Their multivocality enables a wide range of groups and individuals to relate to the same signifier vehicle in a variety of ways. Otherwise hostile groups may form coalitions in political and legal fields by emphasizing different referents of the same "signifier." Jay Abarbanel's and Terence Evens' essays document these statements. Symbols shed and acquire meaning in the passage of time. Myerhoff's and Sherry Turkle's essays provide some exemplification of this process. Wirikuta today, the inverted world of Huichol peyotism, is clearly not what it was in pre-Columbian times, while the barricades set up and the black flags flown during the *événements* of 1968 altered meanings from those of previous Parisian "moments of madness." With this volume comparative symbology becomes firmly linked to processual analysis.

VICTOR TURNER

University of Chicago

Acknowledgments

A number of persons have contributed to the research and writing of this book. First, we owe our students a great deal, especially one cohort of undergraduates who participated in a very stimulating seminar that was an early prelude to *Symbol and Politics*. To Riv-Ellen Prell Foldes, Steven Foldes, Clifford Halenar, Denise Leeper Lawrence, Bruce Murray, Terence Poplawski, Terry Tombs, and Joseph Vasquez we express our gratitude. Eventually a symposium, held at the 1971 meetings of the American Anthropological Association, became the occasion when some of the chapters in this volume were first presented publicly. At that time a number of other papers were given which have to be omitted from this book for lack of space. We mention them here in appreciation of their authors' contributions: Arjun Appadurai, "Bureaucratic Corruption and the Hindi Tradition of Gift-Giving"; David Buchdahl, "The Ideal Community and Its Reality: Patterns of Perception and Denial"; Dorothy Libby, "Conflict Resolution among Selected Siberian Groups"; John Middleton, "The Ideology of Disputes among the Lugbara of Uganda and the Shirazi of Zanzibar"; Carol Swartout, "Goverment for Hire"; Barbara Yngvesson, "Conflict and Communitas: The Maintenance of Egalitarian Norms in a Fishing Community."

Finally, we would like to give special thanks to Julia Kessler for very effective editorial work on the manuscript, and cheerful help in all the chores connected with getting a book to press.

SALLY FALK MOORE
BARBARA G. MYERHOFF

Los Angeles, California

Contents

Prologue

> Every scientific analysis has a specific history, both in the development of the discipline and in the individual development of the research worker.
>
> Gluckman, 1969:373

The history of this book cannot be set down without testimony to the very large presence of Max Gluckman in our lives, and our gratitude to him. Especially important to us have been his years of work cultivating major innovations in the methods of social anthropology, particularly those techniques of microstudy generated by the Manchester School which we all now take for granted. Quite apart from his contributions to the discipline in general, we are specifically grateful for his generous and friendly help in running the symposium of which this book is a product. Our intellectual and personal debt to him is enormous and will never be paid. We dedicate this book to him, recognizing that, like tribal trade-partners, a permanent state of indebtedness was part of the relationship.[1]

Max Gluckman used a number of different approaches to ethnographic material, varying from the most general statements of inferred norms and principles to extremely detailed

[1] We say "was" for just as we were preparing to go to press we received news of his death in Jerusalem on April 14, 1975. He is already much missed and will be long and affectionately remembered by all who knew him. It is with heavy heart that we carry this project through knowing that he will not see it, but we know of no more fitting way to express our personal and professional regard and respect for him.

descriptions of single events. Especially useful to us has been his way of linking particular cases and situations to larger social contexts, to larger theoretical problems, his way of seeing in cases an epitome of such social order as there is. The case or situational method has proved to be as valuable in teaching as in research. We apply it to the collection of cases described in this book, and we applied it to a series of staff-student seminars, the first of which, held in 1970, took as its theme "Ideology and Organization." It was no accident that the initial classroom exercise for the seminar was a discussion of the Lupton and Cunnison article "Workshop Behavior" on the organization of garment workers in Manchester, which appeared in Gluckman's *Closed Systems and Open Minds* (Edinburgh and London, 1964).

The tragic puzzle of South Africa marked Max Gluckman for life. The outward peacefulness and cohesion of the society was for him combined with an early day-to-day knowledge of the bitter underlying oppression and deep schisms. A fascination with complexity, conflict, and contradiction under the mask of apparent cohesion was one of the recurrent themes running through Gluckman's work. In "The Tribal Area in South and Central Africa," he spoke of ideological consensus and structural cohesion in *parts* of the total system. He said: "Clearly . . . consensus and cohesion occur in different areas or in different domains of relationship, and they are present for varying periods of time. . . . These remarks apply also to dissensus and lack of cohesion" (Leo Kuper and M. G. Smith, eds., *Pluralism in Africa*, Berkeley and Los Angeles, 1969:390).

In this book we have sought to approach a limited aspect of this vast topic. Looking at units much smaller than whole societies, we have asked, "How do people committed to an ideology of communal harmony cope with conflict? How is the ideology kept intact?" The problem was posed in a decade of American student interest in "alternative life styles," a decade of horror in Vietnam, a period in which the ideals of peacefulness, egalitarianism, brotherhood, and cooperation were the explicit dogma of collectivities as diverse as apolitical hippie communes and villages committees in Maoist China. Students and faculty alike were particularly aware, at this time of upheaval and confusion, that most dogmatic statements about formal ideologies were not adequate to account for social situations and historical events. The case method was a felicitous tool for research and teaching, because it focused on actual events and on the complex relation between normative ideals and situational adjustments.

In the spring of 1970 the University of Southern California undergraduates in our student-staff seminar did field observations on their own campus and elsewhere in Los Angeles, examining student organizations and other youth groups to consider on a small local scale and on familiar territory the questions raised above.

They looked at everything from the college R.O.T.C. units to a neighborhood commune, from a motorcycle gang to a Japanese sorority. One student observed a fraternity of fellow accounting majors competing for jobs, while another went to the parties of a Chicano gang at which members plotted wars against their black neighbors. Some of these were very new organizations; some were traditional ones. Some had invented their own organizational structure and symbols; others had inherited theirs from previous generations.

Student and youth groups are particularly suitable candidates for study, since their very existence depends on repeated presentations of organizational identity. Every year student groups must recruit new members to replace the ones who have been graduated. New members have to be located in a very large and initially amorphous mass of thousands of students. As a result, there is continuous pressure on student organizations publicly to define their credos, activities, and styles to the potentially recruitable. Other youth groups do the same in the playgrounds of the barrio and in the urban streets.

When the seminar students set out to do their field projects, they were not simply focused on the problem of congruence between organization and ideology. Nor were they simply looking for exciting and shocking disparities between high ideals and low actions. They were looking at organizations to see how they worked, to see on what occasions and in what situations and by what techniques expressions of ideology were made, and what these were. They were observing operating organizations, examining their structure, their activities, and the ideas attached to these. On a very limited but instructive scale, they were looking at the uses of ideology in action. A recurrent range of problems was at once apparent. For example, the necessity for selection in recruiting new members, the embarrassment surrounding expulsion of unwanted individuals, and the reiteration of expressions of collective identity were recognized to be common components of group life. How were these managed to accord with official ideology?

A campus commune provided a rich basis for identifying manipulations of ideology in the face of the problems of daily living. This commune, theoretically anarchistic, publicly claimed, among other things, that all visitors were welcome to stay as long as they liked, that no one should be expelled, and that membership was utterly open. In fact, the commune was troubled regularly by long-term visitors or "crashers" who contributed nothing to group life and drained its resources. No mechanisms or procedures for expulsion existed, since membership selection was "not a problem," because, by fiat, self-selection should have sufficed. Revision of the ideology was assiduously avoided on this critical point. Nevertheless, an especially disliked crasher was firmly ostracized when he approached one of the regular member's girl friends. Sexual possessiveness was tabooed in commune ideology, but in this case it was lower on the hierarchy of values than expulsion of a visitor. After a physical fight between the visitor and the member, the latter was upheld and the former thrown out. This development was explained in terms of individual characteristics—the boyfriend "still had a long way to go" in giving up his sense of sexual possessiveness. At that time the collective pleasure and relief at being rid of the crasher was not acknowledged, and the action was construed as a private rather than a public matter. Some time later, the crasher issue surfaced again and in circumstances that made it impossible for members to deny that de facto expulsions were taking place, and had been for some time. Upon this realization, a group meeting was called, and the members admitted to one another that by supporting and sharing in the ostracism of the visitors they had failed to be true to their beliefs. Rather than confront the necessity for establishing regulations that would violate their ideology on two counts—one, that not everyone was a suitable member, and two, that formal procedures should replace spontaneous, individual motives and desires as a basis for making decisions—they publicly confessed that they had fallen short of their ideals, chastized themselves, and repented, with pledges to try harder in the future. It was a ritual of renewal and an affirmation of ideology, repeated many times in the life of the group.

The commune offered numerous examples of ideology being insulated from the revision necessitated by actual events. The communards were committed to anarchy in procedures as well as beliefs. Impasses occurred often when members were not doing their full share of work spontaneously, or when telephone bills and other mundane realities did not permit everyone to follow his or her own predilections. A regular leader surfaced on such occasions and kept matters in order, but denied that he was leading. All decisions, moreover, had to be unanimous and consensual, according to the ideology of the commune. When in the public meetings no agreement was possible, decisions were simply delayed or postponed as long as possible. When there was no alternative to confrontation and action was imperative, issues would be discussed until most of the concerned individuals were asleep or exhausted, or had departed, so that the few remaining could arrive at a "unanimous decision." At other times, when tension mounted and confrontation with the failure of some of their beliefs seemed inevitable, a different part of their beliefs, not the difficulty at issue, would be dramatized by someone lighting a marijuana cigarette, beginning to sing or play a mutually loved song, breaking into a joke or dance or somehow reminding the others of a cherished moment of cohesiveness in their history —some occasion, perhaps, of making fools out of the enemy. Anger and discomfort would give way to pleasure and camaraderie, for the moment enabling them to avoid the underlying and continuing difficulties besetting their everyday routines.

Several of the groups that were studied claimed more or less anarchistic ideologies and showed similar strains when faced with the necessity for collective action. One case was presented of an outlaw motorcycle gang whose members not only claimed to have no shared beliefs, norms, or procedures, but in fact denied even being a group, since this implied some common affection or at least preference for one another's company, and this was antithetical to their official portrait of themselves as utterly affectless and completely cool. The problem presented here was that even assembling threatened their self-definition, since it demonstrated the presence of social bonds, *ipso facto*. Their solution was to define themselves continually as associates on a negative basis: they were outlaws, detested and persecuted by the outside society. To this end, they contrived events which cast them in the role of the hated and feared enemy of respectable society, and their dress (filthy), public behavior (rowdy and conspicuously defiant), and collective insignia (blatantly iconoclastic, dramatic, and inflammatory) reiterated their position at every turn. Their problem was to disguise all manifestations of mutual support, loyalty, and decency as accidental, meaningless, and due to capricious individual desire rather than social or cultural membership. The forms they used were distinctive, but their problems were the same faced by other groups: how to reconcile their actions with their beliefs. In this case beliefs were reversed in content from that of conventional organizations to show that members always behaved atrociously rather than nobly, but still, so to speak, out of cherished principles. The issue was consistency with collective definition; the processes of symbolic reversal were regular, and only the specific content changed from instance to instance.

A seemingly more conventional organization provided an example no less florid in disguised behavior and manipulation. A student honorary sorority for senior women had a formal set of principles that were issued by the national society indicating clearly the standards for membership in the local chapter, but, characteristically, the criteria set forth were highly general and abstract—girls enlisted were to be "leaders, scholars, contributors to their community and campus." In fact, the local branch operated as a network of friends. It recruited as new members girls described by those already in the group as persons known to be "friendly, popular, beautiful, and fun." Members were selected for social amenities. They were leaders and constituted an élite on their campus and community, but were not chosen on the vague criteria established by the official charter of the society. These were too general to be useful, and in addition were external to the clique which constituted the membership, and not in accord with local standards of leadership. There were few problems in defining any desired girls as "scholars," although they had mediocre grades, since community service could be brought in as a countermeasure. More difficult was the problem of coping with the mechanisms for member selection, which were very specific and intended to distinguish between mere social sororities and the scholastic sorority. Blackballing was forbidden as an unsuitable practice for recruitment to this organization, and nominations were to be by former members and faculty, and finally acted upon in open voting. The girls manipulated this situation by an "informal" discussion prior to the official selection session in which blackballing indeed took place. At the informal session, never officially called or recorded, needed information was exchanged, decisions covertly made, and consensus established; when the official afternoon meeting began, members were ready to vote in the open. No one explicitly acknowledged any overriding of official criteria by means of this arrangement. All remained in good standing with the national organization, in collusive good faith with one another.

The harvest of the student seminar gave impetus to pursue the problem further. A professional symposium was proposed for which it was decided to narrow the focus by holding constant a single segment of an ideology: the commitment to communal harmony. In the face of this conviction, how did people regulate their affairs, deal with conflict, inconsistency, and the like? Since we knew that communal harmony was an ideal attractive to groups that had quite opposite views of how it should be achieved: through regulation and planning or through the absence of rules and the cultivation of individuality, spontaneity, freedom, and openness, we decided to solicit such materials, and to inspect cases collected by trained anthropologists in their fieldwork, using our own fieldwork as a core.

Such a symposium was held at the 1971 meeting of the American Anthropological Association in New York City, when it was proposed

to identify and analyze some of the techniques and forms by means of which ideals of communal harmony are preserved in the face of potentially divisive disputes. The management of conflict situations in planned communities having explicit ideologies of cooperation, such as communes and kibbutzim, is compared with the management of disputes in lineages and other "unplanned" or "traditional" social units. Strategies employed in reconciling the actuality of conflict with the ideology of cooperation are examined in these two different social contexts.

The symposium was chaired with characteristic flair by Max Gluckman. It started off with a broad and stimulating analytic overview on the classification of ideologies, delivered by Victor Turner. We were disappointed that his introduction could not be included in this volume; our reliance on his work and our gratitude for his encouragement are evident in the papers.

The present volume reflects a somewhat different emphasis from the stated purpose of the 1971 symposium. Our focus has shifted to the problem of regulation and situational adjustment. The communities treated here vary little in idealizing a general communal harmony, but vary considerably as to their conception of how that ideal is to be achieved. They differ as to whether it is to be reached by means of planning, that is, through the use of regular rules and procedures, or by means of voluntary spontaneous agreement. The *kibbutz* and the *moshav* are ideologically committed to the notion that the source of conflict in society is essentially economic (see the chapters by Abarbanel and Evens). These Israeli communities approach the solution of economic problems by means of planning and rules, believing as they do that genuine individual freedom can be achieved only through the regulation of society. They are "intentional communities," consciously committed to ordering their way of life, to meeting problems with thought-out solutions, with "rationally" achieved rules and procedures. They epitomize the planned community.

At the other end of the spectrum are collectivities like some communes and movements committed to an *antiplanned* way of life, to a do-your-own-thing conception of individual freedom, and to spontaneous resolution of whatever problems arise. In between those whose poles are planned or antiplanned are such groups as the Chagga of Kilimanjaro, and the Huichol of Mexico in their ordinary life as farmers. Their traditional communities are not ideologically committed to planning or to antiplanning. Choices, individual and collective, are certainly recognized to exist as matters of practical necessity. But these choices are not complicated by extreme idealization of the spontaneous acts of individuals, or by very strong feelings of faith in the efficacy of planning. Instead, daily life takes place against the background of a traditional order, associated with a past time, recognized as having been modified by changing circumstances but in some very general sense accepted as the proper way of doing things. In some groups where reliance on traditional systems is much talked about, the actual behavioral emphasis is on the achievement of apparent public consensus rather than on conformity to given norms. In contrast, in both of the two symposium case studies which concern temporary aggregations of people instead of communities (being the cases of the French students and the Woodstock youth), spontaneity and an absence of tradition or plan are idealized. A diagrammatic representation of the ideological continuum embodied in the symposium papers might look like this:

Regularization idealized .... to .... Indeterminacy idealized

Planned intentional communities	*Regulated but nonplanned traditional communities*	*Antiplanned community, aggregate, or situation*
Kibbutzim	Chagga	French students
Moshavim	Huichol	Woodstock youth
		Hippie commune

This classification may prove useful in future studies. Anthropological material describing traditional societies abounds. In fact, most anthropological literature is of this kind. Examples of planned communities are also plentiful, but more studies are needed, especially in the socialist/communist world. As for the antiplanned collectivities discussed here, one is impelled to ask whether they were an aberration of the 1960s or the expression of a recurrent attitude that can be expected to reappear? We offer here the beginning of a framework for considering these questions.

PART ONE

THE IDEALIZATION
OF SPONTANEITY

Introduction to Part One

Intentional communities may be designed with the view that only through rational, careful planning and social and self-regulation will the causes of conflict be eliminated and communal harmony attained. Alternatively, designers of communities may conclude that the best government is the least government. In this view, people left to their own devices will live peaceably, and instead of regulation and planning, freedom and spontaneity are the means for reaching their goal. Both interpretations have difficulties. The first must contend with the inevitable appearance of disorder, societal and personal, and the latter is threatened by spontaneous emergence of order and structure. Two of the cases that follow (Woodstock and the French student uprising) present societies, groups, and movements which regard regulation itself as anathema to their goals. They are rather extreme examples of anti-planning elevated to the level of an ideology. Regularity and repetitiveness are threatening to their ideology and must be manipulated and interpreted—in terms of it—as accidents, misunderstandings, or personal failures which do not call into question the premises on which their way of life is founded. Paradoxically, in these groups, people frequently regulate against regulation, and this presents some highly interesting stratagems and maneuvers. Since by definition it is impossible for them to acknowledge their manipulations, one finds a florescence of unacknowledged arrangements for conducting their daily affairs. Dispute management, decision making, leadership, compromise, division of labor—indeed all kinds of regulatory procedures and administrative mechanisms become matters of disguise, subterfuge, self-deception, conscious and unconscious collusion.

Collective action presents great difficulties to groups with an antiplanning ideology. The carrying out of complex projects that require coordination, subordination of individual desires, and delayed gratification is highly problematic, especially in those groups which aspire to provide members with a complete way of life. Communes based on an antiplanning ideology in which people live full-time must struggle continually with ways of taking action and legislating affairs. Some of these difficulties have been touched on in connection with the campus commune described by one of the seminar students. There, for example, the group leader was also the founder and held the mortgage for the home in which the commune was housed. His leadership and financial direction were presented as accidental, due to his facility with figures, and not in the least reflective of any regulatory or structural considerations. And, again, the communards in the Woodstock case attributed social distinctions to differences in degrees of successful socialization—which were interpreted as representing temporary vestiges of the insidious influence of life outside.

The time factor is always an important consideration. The Huichol pilgrims, French students, and Woodstock youth represent time-out-of-life episodes, variations of the periods of license and carnival which are common in societies of all sorts. And for a short period of time, it is possible to achieve communal harmony through the spontaneity and freedom they venerate. As temporary aggregates, they need not cope with normal societal imperatives, and they can afford to idealize spontaneity. They need not occupy themselves with the production and distribution of goods, the getting and spending, the enduring modes of cooperation. Nor do they handle dispute, certainly one of the inevitable problems confronting any permanent community. Indeed, among the Huichols, the setting aside of interpersonal antagonisms and discord for the duration of their pilgrimage is one of the expressions of their view of that experience as a special, even sacred occasion, not meant to endure. The pilgrimage is a time set apart by the very fact that everything in it is supposed to be the opposite of the normal order. The pilgrims act out a systematic suspension of ordinary reality and regulation despite the highly structured and traditional nature of the journey. For all its antiorderly ideology and all its declared seeking after individual freedom, personal fulfillment, and private visions, the pilgrimage is a very orderly collective occurrence, governed by clear, even rigid, rules. It is a culturally regularized escape from the here and now of everyday life—of being born, living, working, struggling, dying in the mundane world.

By contrast, both the Woodstock youth and the French students achieve their exhilarated communal assemblage only once, in a single, short-lived eruption of fervent emotion, a phenomenon that Turner calls "spontaneous communitas" (Turner, *The Ritual Process*, Chicago, 1969:131). During these heightened episodes, they are also declaring themselves to epitomize the opposite of the normal order. As ephemeral as their coming together may be, their vision is of a millennium when such brotherly sentiments and collaborative actions might flourish permanently. This ideal of a communal harmony so perfect that it is the opposite of the normal order seems much more plausible when those enjoying it are carefully segregated from ordinary societal concerns. Thus through certain special events did the French students and the Woodstock young people briefly achieve a euphoric sense of total and lasting communal harmony: the millennium had arrived.

And, it must be recognized that none of these three cases (Woodstock, Huichol, and French students) represents a total or autonomous social entity. That they are all small parts of larger social wholes has twofold significance. First, these groups are in varying degrees politically and economically dependent on the larger world around them. Without the external support received from outside their own group, they would be even more abbreviated in size, scope, and temporal existence. Second, they are shaped ideologically in terms of their opposition to the outside: in a sense they are communities of opposition. For them, the ideal of communal harmony within is understood in terms of strife and antagonism without. The outside world re-enters periodically in many forms and is interpreted as polluting their life and endangering their goals. Internal troubles of all kinds are explained in terms of the corrupt values of the surrounding society. The rejection of the normal social order may find expression in the rejection of order per se, as it does for the Woodstock people and French students. Rejection of the structure and values of a particular society is thus enlarged into a rejection of all structure, all fixed order, all set rules. This ideology of antiplanning may be all-encompassing, but as we have seen, it is weak in providing guides to action, except for instances when it suggests action in terms of opposition to the prevailing rules. The resultant paralysis of action is bearable in delimited circumstances but in the long run has disastrous results. This appeared in many of the student seminar studies that dealt with different kinds of anti-ideology youth groups, from a free clinic which attempted to run a program on a hang-loose basis that could not schedule medical appointments, given its ideology, to the efforts of the motorcycle gang when it decided to buy identifying group jackets. When action was managed, it was through the kinds of stratagems which allowed members to claim that their choices were spontaneously determined rather than planned, collective decisions.

Some of the specific stratagems employed by the antiplanning social forms are illuminating. We have touched on the disguise which is made in the form of claiming regularity to be accidental, reflecting individual pecularities and talents. Regularities are construed to be one-of-a-kind events, particularized so as to have no implications for the ideology. A variation on this theme was the interpretation of behaviors as manifestations of accidents. Decisions can be arrived at by the use of I Ching, and group antagonisms can be viewed as reflecting mysterious, supernatural forces of all sorts, from witchcraft to Jungian typologies. All events provide explanations which side-step attribution of predictability and do not carry the implication of possible remedy through design, intention, or planning, since accident and destiny are beyond human, rational control. The affinity for surrealism in art is another manifestation of the preference for understandings which appear in accidental configurations, underscoring the non-sense of life and relationships.

Short-lived encounters, postponements, simple collective projects, and the use of drugs to provide retreat into subjectivity are frequently used in avoiding conflict, but result in an adumbrated, much-limited social life. Self-help also appears in individual crises in lieu of group regulatory procedures, but requires no collective interpretation. Issues are also avoided by ad hominem analyses which attribute them to personal idiosyncrasies. When confrontations with failure are not avoidable, communards, for example, developed rituals of contrition which become occasions for reaffirming rather than questioning their ideology. Purge and purification rites, often conducted in group therapylike sessions, effectively refocused attention on particularities of people and events. Inevitably, contaminating outside influences would be cited, and pledges to throw them off more assiduously consolidated rather than threatened ideological commitment. Ambiguity was employed in various forms in avoiding confrontations that threatened the ideology. The devaluation of logic, reason, and precise verbal communication, the stress on permissiveness, and the use of symbolism to convey messages were also useful in by-passing awareness of conflicts or differences. Thus a complex, often ingenious, range of stratagems replaced procedures. This is not to attribute an exceptional malevolence or dishonesty among adherents to the ideology of antiplanning. All people guard their beliefs and contrive to interpret their behaviors as consonant with and expressive of them. Regularities in masking regularity are no more than a vocabulary appropriate to these kinds of groups and movements, and in other belief systems different accommodations can be found. It is our task here to bring out some of the forms particular to these cases and leave to others the identification of idioms of adjustment suitable to other explanatory beliefs.

CHAPTER 1

Organization and Ecstasy: Deliberate and Accidental Communitas among Huichol Indians and American Youth

BARBARA G. MYERHOFF

The term "communitas," as used by Victor Turner, refers to a type of interpersonal relationship that may and does occur almost anywhere and in all kinds of societies—complex and simple, archaic and modern, unplanned and planned. This usage of communitas differs from the historical, temporal, and spatial limits usually implied by "community," and emphasizes that communitas is not limited to communities and is not necessarily more intense or common in that or any other given social type of relationship.

Communitas is only comprehensible in terms of "structure," which is its opposite; indeed communitas is "antistructure." By structure, Turner is not referring to statistical outcomes or unconscious categories, following the usages of some anthropologists. Instead he refers to the frame of social order that consists in a system of roles, statuses, and positions occupied by individuals through time.

Of analytic importance here is the social personality or persona, not the unique individual, not the concrete human being. This is because in communitas, social structure is suspended—group life is homogeneous and undifferentiated, therefore the whole man matters. His social roles do not.

Structure is always necessary for the maintenance of group life. By means of it, work is organized and accomplished in a predictable and orderly manner, and this takes place through the allocation of labor and responsibility—in other words, through role differentiation. But the very existence of these roles and the impersonal limits that they impose prevents the emergence of communitas. It is only when the whole man is permitted to act spontaneously, without social responsibility and accountability, that communitas can develop. By definition, communitas cannot take place within structure, for it is ecstatic, literally an escape from the self. The spirit, in soaring flight, is liberated from the body and, correspondingly, from the social and historical rootedness that provides the daily mortal context.[1] Of course, no one remains in a state of ec-

---

[1] From time to time Turner speaks of "raw" as opposed to "domesticated" or "routinized" communitas. I have departed here from his usage, for I find the contradiction too deep to manage. Throughout this chapter, I am using communitas as *not* routinized, mild, or mundane, but always as intense, passionate, and totally involving its participants. While communitas may be "structured" in the sense of being orderly, planned for, anticipated, patterned, and even organized, it is never routine or affectively neutral. It may be embedded in and surrounded by ritual, but if it is ritualized *and* mundane, it is not communitas.

It must be recognized that though communitas and structure are treated as entirely opposed, ultimately they differ in terms of degree not kind. All human activity is patterned in some measure, including the most wildly aberrant activities we may conceive. A given society and its participants may perceive such activities as absolutely chaotic and unprecedented, but the outside analyst sees cultural influences. What is important is that the actors themselves define a situation as ecstatic and spontaneous, however predictable it may be found to be by the observer. Thus the "real self" is not sensibly separable from the

stasy indefinitely, so there must be ways of entering and leaving this condition, paths, as it were, between communitas and structure. Some societies provide such paths and chart the passages, and others leave them to chance, a risky business as will be seen.

In communitas, men involve their most private selves totally with one another and without the slightest suggestion of purpose or instrumentality. This is what Buber called *Zwischenmenschlichkeit*, and it is a transformative, often mystical experience. Without communitas, man and society are incomplete; yet without structure, existence is impossible. Dazzled by the power and joy of communitas, men often come together and attempt to institutionalize this condition by establishing utopian societies, but these efforts flounder when, as Turner (1969) puts it, "men find that they have to produce life's necessities through work . . . to mobilize resources." To mobilize resources means to mobilize people, and eventually to return to structural segmentation and hierarchy. The production and distribution of resources results in a return to structure sooner or later. When instrumental concerns must be handled, delegation of labor and responsibilities reappears, along with deferment of gratification and treatment of the other fellow as a part of a larger task rather than an end in himself. The group finds itself back in organizational modality. To everyone's consternation ecstasy is gone. This is the dialectical relationship between structure and communitas, the fluctuation between joy and duty that constitutes the ceaseless flow of social life. Getting stuck at either pole and neglecting the existence and importance of the other are fatal: a dynamic

---

"social self," just as human nature cannot really be known apart from culture. We are dealing here with folk categories, whether conscious or unconscious, and not with eternal realities.

equilibrium between the two poles is the only viable arrangement.

Deliberate and Accidental Communitas

Throughout history efforts have been made to sustain and institutionalize communitas as a permanent way of life. Usually in the form of utopian societies or communes, these efforts have met with varying success and failure, encountered predictable difficulties, and employed recurring techniques for coping with the re-emergence of structure. Experiments in sustained communitas, though important areas of study, are not taken up in this chapter. Here my concern is with comparing two examples of intermittent communitas—in one case communitas is accidental, spontaneous and ad hoc; in the other, deliberate and organized. How can communitas be planned and regulated without being routinized? How do the remembrance and anticipation of communitas affect individual and group life? What are the dangers of haphazard communitas occurring without socially provided maps, time tables, and interpretations? These are some of the questions illuminated by the contrasting cases.

The example of accidental communitas used here is "Woodstock," a reference to the florescence of American youth culture during the middle and late 1960's, known variously as "the counterculture," "hippie culture," "flower power," the "Woodstock Nation," and so forth. The high point of this movement was thought by many to have occurred in the summer of 1968 at an outdoor rock-music festival in Woodstock, New York. It lasted four days, was attended by approximately 500,000 young people, and was widely seen as constituting the fullest realization of the group's most cherished values. In this case, Woodstock provides an excellent example of ad hoc communitas. It never recurred, at least not with the same intensity or in the same proportions, and the memory of it, the confusion and grief over its loss, made a considerable contribution to the ultimate dissolution of the Nation. In this interpretation, Woodstock became a kind of lost paradise, haunting and elusive to its devotees, both for those who had actually been there and for those who knew it vicariously and mythically.

The example of deliberate communitas is provided by the Huichol Indians of North Central Mexico, whose pilgrimages to Wirikuta also constitute a quest for a remembered paradise and a realization of communitas. Like Woodstock, Wirikuta is a real place, a myth, and a symbol. Geographically, Wirikuta is a desert region situated several hundred miles away from the Huichols' habitat, a place of their origins, mythically and in all likelihood historically.

Dissimilar in so many ways, Woodstock and Wirikuta are alike, nevertheless, in that both have come to symbolize a vanished Eden, drawing pilgrims in quest of the sacred past. For the Huichol pilgrims, Wirikuta represents Ancient Times —the way things were in the primordial beginning, when men were gods, and the way things will be once more after the world ends. For the hippie, Woodstock is a recent past, when "the Nation" convened its multitudes in joy and beauty, a time-out-of-life which showed that their visions were realizable programs for the future. The most significant difference between the two Edenic quests is that the Huichol version of paradise really can be regained. But for the hippie, paradise is a haunting dream. The Huichol pilgrim finds his mundane life enriched by his memories of Wirikuta and anticipates another return with joy. Woodstock is a nonrecurrent event. The hippie pilgrim is left perplexed by his recollections of lost communion, and his everyday burdens are more trivial and onerous than ever in the shadow of his memories of Woodstock.

In this interpretation, the difference is attributable to two distinct but related factors: the Woodstock quest is haphazard, and Woodstock is perceived as representing a vision of the permanent and natural condition of mankind. In contrast to the hippie pilgrims, the Huichols have orderly procedures for entering and leaving Wirikuta. They accept its evanescent, episodic character, and are aware that in this world mortals cannot hope to dwell in Wirikuta permanently. It seems then that the consequences of consciously seeking and designing communities are enormous. Let us consider the deliberate communitas of the Huichol in more detail.

Wirikuta: Deliberate Communitas[2]

The Huichol Indians are a quasi-tribe of mountain-dwelling maize agriculturalists numbering perhaps 10,000 and representing one of the least acculturated groups in Mexico. It is their cluster of religious ceremonies, symbols, and myths concerned with their annual pilgrimages to Wirikuta, the home of the First People, that is of major interest here. Under the leadership of a shaman-priest (the *mara'akame*), a small group of pilgrims go on these occasions to "hunt the peyote" in the high desert region of San Luis Potosi, several hundred miles from their present homeland in the Sierra Madre Occidental. At the climactic moment of the ceremony, a fusion is achieved

---

[2] The following observations are drawn from field work carried out from 1966 to the present. Huichol religious and symbolic processes are examined in detail in *Peyote Hunt* (1974), and in "The Deer-Maize-Peyote Symbol Complex Among the Huichol Indians of Mexico" (1970), both by Barbara G. Myerhoff.

on many levels: historical, sociological, and psychological. Men merge with one another in a seamless, ecstatic continuity, overcoming all significant divisions and barriers—between people, adult and child, man and woman, leader and follower, between plant and animal, man and nature, man and the deities, between past, present, and future, between the "lived-in" order and the "dreamed-in" order. "It is all one, it is a unity, it is ourselves," they say of this cataclysmic moment. It is a recovery of the Beginning, before time began and the original wholeness of the cosmos was divided into the categories of life's present forms, and it is an anticipation of how things shall be at the end of time when all is put back together again.

The return to Wirikuta appears to be a return to a historical as well as mythical homeland and way of life. A growing and consistent body of evidence suggests that the Huichol lived as hunters and gatherers in this region and that various pressures forced their retreat to the mountains and their relatively recent adoption of a sedentary, agricultural way of life.[3] In their own traditions, the Huichols were driven out of Wirikuta when they were still semidivine Ancient Ones, and in this form they return, becoming themselves the gods retracing their path to the sacred place where "all is one." The essence of this return takes the form of the peyote hunt, where a fusion occurs between the deer, representing their romantic, nomadic, free, hunting past; the maize, symbolizing the hardships and necessities of the mundane present; and the

[3] For a detailed treatment of the ethnobotanical, mythical, archeological, and cultural historical evidence on which is based the hypothesis that Wirikuta is the homeland of Huichols, in fact as well as in mythical tradition, see Peter T. Furst and Barbara G. Myerhoff (1966).

peyote, evoking the timeless, purposeless, private vision of beauty which mediates between deer and maize, providing the Huichol with the experience of being one people despite the drastic changes in their recent history, society, and culture.[4] All the contradictions and paradoxes contained within this sacred symbol complex are embraced and transcended during the peyote hunt.

The safety of the pilgrims is the sole responsibility and burden of the *mara'akame*, and for this he studies and trains many years. He tests and demonstrates aptitude for his sacred profession in this ceremony, for the full-fledged *mara'akame* must undertake the leadership of five such yearly journeys. Until he had done this, "he has not completed himself." The days preceding and following the actual journey are crowded with ceremonies of preparation and conclusion.

The pilgrims cannot enter Wirikuta as mortals. They must be transformed into the Ancient Ones, and in this the *mara'akame* assists them by "dreaming" their deity names and informing them of their godly identities. He undertakes numerous severe privations throughout the ceremony and leads the pilgrims in doing so as well; sexual relations, bathing, normal eating, drinking, and sleeping—all are foresworn during the pilgrimage, for these are the requirements of mortal life. Early in the preparations for traveling to Wirikuta is a ceremony which might be called "knotting-in." Here, a cord symbolizing the unity of the party is circulated and a knot made for each pilgrim. All are bonded together in "complete affection and trust," for without this "giving their hearts to

---

[4] The function of peyote in bridging distinct historical periods, thus providing a phenomenological sense of being the same people, in the past and present, was suggested by Craig Calhoun of Los Angeles in a personal communication (1971).

each other and the *mara'akame"* the latter is powerless to protect them. In still another ceremony preceding the pilgrimage, each member of the group "confesses" his illicit sexual exploits and is cleansed of these by the *mara'akame*. The cleansing returns the individual to a condition of childlike innocence, symbolizing his purity of heart and body and his utter devotion to his fellow pilgrims. Following purification and instruction, the pilgrims are given another set of deity names (renaming occurs several times during the course of the journey) and are reborn as the Ancient Ones.

The pilgrims retrace the departure of the Ancient Ones from Wirikuta, re-enacting their adventures. The trip is not arduous for them as deities, but as mortals they make many sacrifices. These parties of Indians often walk out of the Sierra to their destination, a venture which takes several weeks and covers several hundred miles. Even when they travel by bus or truck, the trip remains strenuous because of the many privations necessitated by their sacred condition.

Sometime before the party of pilgrims actually enters the Sacred Land, everything is equated with its opposite and then reversed. The known world is backwards and upside down.[5] The old man becomes the little child. That which is sad and ugly is spoken of as beautiful and gay. One thanks another by telling him, "You are welcome." One greets another by turning his back on him and bidding him goodbye. The sun is the moon, the moon the sun; it is said that "the moon is brighter

---

[5] Such systems of reversal are not unusual in classical mythology or ethnographic accounts. Both Jung (1946) and Eliade (1962) have demonstrated how often reversals or symbolic inversions are used to suggest the union of opposites. The mystery of cosmic totality (*coincidentia oppositorum*) is an extremely widespread religious concern, as Eliade has shown. For a more detailed discussion, see Barbara G. Myerhoff (1976).

there [in Wirikuta], the sun darker, so that both are the same. They are each other. And so it will be again when the world ends." This is a ritual enactment of the fusion of oppositions. Thus are the separations which began with creation mended there in Wirikuta.

The great danger facing the pilgrims in this paradisial state is the temptation to linger there. Literally, this can be fatal, for the *kupüri* or "soul thread" which binds each individual to the particular deity who puts life into him, may be severed, and the soul could not then return to the body. Each wishes to stay, having been told of Wirikuta all his life, having since childhood participated in rituals which celebrate its beauties and benefits. But immediately after the successful hunting and eating of the first peyote, the *mara'akame* leads his group away, beyond the danger of this cosmic unification, back into the structure of everyday life. Reluctantly, the pilgrims follow him out, weeping, running, lamenting the loss of what they have so long yearned for and known for so short a time.

Elaborate precautions must be taken so that not the tiniest part of Wirikuta is left on the body or clothes of the pilgrim. Each one is ritually cleansed of every bit of dirt or cactus spine, and the pilgrim carries out of Wirikuta remnants of all that he ate or drank there. Thus boundaries are scrupulously observed; the things of the sacred and the everyday are kept apart rigidly.[6] Even the pilgrims' deity names are left behind, and the new names are given for the trip home. And finally, at the edge of the Sacred Land, a ritual undoing of their unity

---

[6] Mary Douglas (1966) elaborates on such separations in her discussion of pollution and purity. Sacred things and places are defiled by contact with the nonsacred and must be rigidly segregated. Or, as Lévi-Strauss put it (1966), that which is in its proper place is sacred *because* it is in its proper place, not the converse.

is conducted by the *mara'akame*, who removes from the cord the knots which had originally been placed there to symbolize the devotion and connection of the pilgrims to each other. Thus all remnants and traces of the experience are left behind. The pilgrims bid each other goodbye, grieving for the loss of the Sacred Land and the most intense comradeship they are ever to know. It is understood that their union does not belong to the realm of the everyday and is not to be perverted for mundane purposes. No enduring or stable alliances are generated as a result of the pilgrimage. Pilgrims do not expect or owe mutual aid to each other in the future. Their bonds are spiritual and ritual, and of the past, without implying duties or rights. Thus there can be no disappointment or tarnishing of the sacred experience by the everyday secular contacts.[7]

Pilgrims and *mara'akame* alike stress the perils of Wirikuta. Why is it dangerous to go there? Why suffer such hardships only to depart almost immediately? The lure of Wirikuta lies in the wish to deny the place of structure in life and the attempt to replace it by total and sustained communitas. In its most exaggerated and complete form, communitas is a loss of self, a fusion of the individual with the group, the cosmos, the womb, or whatever image one prefers to use to signify the loss of adult separateness and accountability. Only a shaman can enjoy the privilege of ready access to the communitas of First Times, and his training for this profession is as rigorous

[7] It is hoped by all that they may one day return to *Wirikuta* together, but this is rare. Occasionally a few people do so, but within the context of a different grouping, often lead by a different *mara'akame*. Ideally, on returning home the *mara'akame* builds a circle of oratories to symbolize each of the deities who journeyed to Wirikuta that year together, but these serve merely as reminders and are not a base for collective action.

as his talents and status are unique in society; only he is permitted freely to come and go between this ordinary world and the other sacred realms.

Many philosophical and psychological systems have dealt with this most extreme form of communitas; the Jungians handled it within the concept of uroboric incest, a state in which the individual refuses to differentiate and become adult. The Freudians conceptualized the notion as a form of the desire to return to the womb, or the wish never to have been separated at all from prenatal dependence and blissful unconsciousness.[8] Whatever metaphor one prefers, the danger is the same. It is the refusal to accept the human condition, to suffer, die, be alone—to be mortal. The danger is that one will lose his soul (rationality, volition, *kupüri*, ego, and so forth), will cling to communitas and will not wish or be able to return to everyday life. He will be struck at one pole of existence, attempting to choose ecstasy as a permanent way of life.

Here the *mara'akame* must protect those in his care from their own yearnings and frailty. He is well trained and well equipped for this responsibility. He draws on a body of tradition, in the form of myth, ceremony, and symbol through which he assists the pilgrim in attaining and then relinquishing paradise, allowing them to experience ecstasy and then return

---

[8] The entrance into Wirikuta is attained between clashing rocks, through a gate known as The Vagina. This may be interpreted as supporting a Freudian interpretation of the pilgrimage as a return to the womb or re-entry into the Earth Mother. But it is well to remember that such symbolic interpretations are artifacts of the Western mind. For the Huichol, distinctions between sociological and psychological levels do not exist; theirs is a total system which does not necessitate analogies. Wirikuta is *itself*—a total unity, containing multiple irreducible realities. It is erroneous to interpret it as symbolic of anything else.

to organization. The *mara'akame* leads the Huichols in and out of an intermittent communitas, and he helps them accept the transient nature of the experience, so that it enhances their ordinary lives, buttresses a stable social system, and vivifies the part each individual plays in maintaining the totality of his society and culture. The Huichols say that their symbols make them rich, and indeed the continuing possibility of re-entering paradise gives them the reality as well as the myth of returning to primordial unity. There is no doubt but that this accounts in large part for the Huichols' insistence that their way of life is the most beautiful there is. They cherish and cling to the religious system which allows them access to paradise in this life.

Woodstock: Accidental Communitas[9]

"Woodstock pilgrims" is used here to refer to a group of young people who designated themselves variously as, "hip-

[9] The following interpretation is based on fieldwork conducted during the summer of 1970 and 1971. It consisted of group discussions, lengthy interviews (structured and open-ended), and participant observation with about thirty university students between the ages of 18 and 25. I had known these people for about two years before we began our formal discussions and had the opportunity to follow rather closely the emergence and development of their ideology and life style. We came together in the summers for the express purpose of examining the content of their subculture and what happened to it when implemented and sustained. In other words, the students were engaged in self-study, and were serious in their desire to comprehend their own lives and the events which impinged upon them. Customarily, they analyzed their own activities and values and kept track of "the movement," in its broadest extension, that is, the variations on counterculture activities as practiced by their friends and acquaintances all over the country, and as reported by their extended networks and in the media. Many kept journals diligently; some kept files of newspaper and magazine clippings, and notes on their collective experiences and interpretations. All liked to engage in endless discussions about

pies," "freaks," "flower children," "acid heads," members of the "movement," "tribe," "nation," "revolution," or "counterculture." Not all had attended Woodstock, the event, but all were Woodstock pilgrims in a cultural sense; all held Woodstock as a cherished symbol and validation of their chosen way of life. Their nostalgia and grief over the nonrecurrence of the event impelled them to attempt to recover it. It is because of their quest for the lost communion of Woodstock that they are regarded here as pilgrims.

What is it that Woodstock stood for? For this group, it was a period of mass ecstasy and a somewhat miraculous event. It drew together an astoundingly large assemblage, and, without organization or detailed planning, it provided an atmosphere of spontaneity and harmony, in a joining together that was orderly without structure, anarchic but not chaotic. All this appeared to occur as a result of unspoken sharing, good will, and commonality. It was communitas for a protracted period of time and on an unprecedented scale, with good will flowing miraculously from every person there "doing his own thing in his own way." The event was a

---

what was happening to them and their life-style over time, and their self-consciousness was inestimably valuable in making it possible to appraise the meaning and impact of Woodstock over time.

The size of the group with which I worked makes it necessary to limit generalizations. Nevertheless, this group had contacts with a great many people like themselves, and often spoke for them. Part of their calendar of activities included fixed and regular rounds—certain people, campuses, crash pads, communes, demonstrations, rallies, festivals, and drug contacts—which were essential contact points on the itinerary. In this manner a far-flung communication network was sustained, and cultural diffusion operated efficiently and rapidly. Accordingly, there is reason to believe that the yearning for Woodstock described here characterized many more people than those with whom I worked directly.

stupendous experience, a sign that their utopian fantasies were realizable, indeed were actually happening! It meant that "good vibes" *really could* replace social organization as a modus vivendi, for the tribe, for the nation, for everybody in the world. The young people weren't crazy utopian romantic children as their parents and teachers had claimed: adults were cynical and wrong, and Woodstock proved it.[10]

From Woodstock on, however, it was downhill, terminating only two years later with the rock festival at Altamont, California, which was disaster on every count. Short-lived, violent, ugly, frightening, it brought a general consensus that the days of innocent flower-power-all-you-need-is-love were over forever. Many explanations for this loss were offered by the young people during our discussions; too many "hard cubes" had gone down in the interim (LSD had recently become illegal and the immediate effect was "hard cubes," and bad trips due to low-quality drugs); too much political hassling and police interference had occurred, which led to the recognition that "people won't let you do your own thing," and that cultural innovations, even without accompanying desires to introduce change in anyone else's life, were threatening and treated as political acts. Much of the content of counterculture life-style had become trendy and commercialized by Madison Avenue. By 1970, "Haight was over" (Haight-Ashbury was the district of San Francisco which had been the focus of the West Coast flower-power movement), "People's Park was lost" (the improvised neighborhood park in Berkeley which had been illegally established by students and street people on University land and was closed by the police), and all major rock festivals and halls had closed down.

[10] For a detailed discussion of the symbolic significance of Woodstock, see Abbie Hoffman (1969).

"Tribal gatherings" of any size seemed to end in violence and confrontations with police or hostile neighbors. The very anticipation of these difficulties, the "bad vibrations" they aroused, spoiled the possibility of achieving communitas.

The meaning of Woodstock and its loss can be understood only by placing it in the context of the pilgrims' ideology and social organization, for in this context the significance and centrality of communitas becomes clear.

The social organization of the group I worked with during 1970 and 1971 can be described briefly as a widely ramified, unstable, overlapping, loosely articulated series of networks, with very little internal social differentiation apart from esteem accorded to individuals informally because of special talents (usually in the areas of musical ability, high personal style, or political sophistication). In general, counterculture people share certain known sociological and biographical characteristics (i.e., Caucasian, middle and upper-middle socioeconomic class background, politically liberal persuasions, some college or university training with interest in liberal arts and humanities, etc. [Bell and Kristol, 1968]). They comprise, for the most part, a social category that acts as a group only occasionally, but those participants experience a sense of common history, social location, shared basic values, preferred lifestyles, and ultimate goals. Despite the shifting nature of the population, members who participate in this cultural network can quickly and easily form into groups, due to a well-developed sense of common identity based on a rich and complex body of symbols, rituals, and insignia that enable them to locate and contact their fellows among multitudes of strangers.

The ideology has been touched on. The counterculture ethos was a fascinating combination of political goals (the movement) and cultural goals (flower power). It was a two-pronged program at odds with itself, the life-style or cultural side in opposition to the political side.[11] Briefly, the cultural goals called for a way of life which is the very essence of communitas: affectively intense, direct, with totally engrossing interpersonal relations; behaviors which are nonutilitarian but spontaneous, expressive, and immediate; equilitarian, undelegated, status-free arrangements for common action; dependence on intuition, emotion, and accident as the ultimate and authoritative sources of wisdom; emphasis on that which is simple, natural, basic, sensually pleasurable and concrete in matters of aesthetics and morality. Other major ideological concerns included valuing timeless, causeless, flowing experiences, and in sexual matters, a tendency to minimize sex differentiation; interest in "the primitive," in peasant, rural, tribal, folk or ethnic themes as genuine, in contrast to what was regarded as artificial in commerce, urbanism, and civilization; disregard for personal appearance and disdain for clothing which might indicate differentiated, hierarchical positions in society, as well as a profound interest in the bizarre, surreal, ambiguous, and haphazard. All these are themes which constitute some of the cultural dimensions of their ideology.[12]

[11] See Barbara G. Myerhoff (1971), for an analysis of this duality.

[12] The values emphasized by counterculture ideology are evidently stable concerns among the various kinds of people whom Turner (1969) has called liminal, that is, on the margins of society. The quest for communitas is often a concern to people who fall outside of or in between the established statuses and categories of a social order. For a fuller discussion of the relationship between communitas and liminality, the reader is referred especially to "Liminality and Communitas," "Communitas: Model and Process," and "Humility and Hierarchy: The Liminality of Status Elevation and Reversal," in Turner, *The Ritual Process* (pp. 94–203).

In this discussion, I have interpreted communitas as an escape from structure and from self, an Edenic condition of communion and unity. In various of his writings, Turner uses communitas more broadly and flexibly than this.

Their political program, on the other hand, called for concrete social changes, often on a massive scale, involving redistribution of wealth and power, alterations in foreign policy, the dismantling of entire institutions, and so forth. This side of their program required organization, hierarchical arrangements, delegation of authority and responsibility, delayed gratification, role differentiation and allocation. It necessitated self-restraint, instrumentality in orientation, and all the deception, compartmentalization, and calculation which are routine features of political tactics and strategies.

Obviously these two programs of the Revolution were in opposition, comprising an unresolvable paradox. In the abstract, of course, there was little need to confront this paradox, but in action situations it did emerge repeatedly and was dealt with in various ways, most commonly by the evocation of potent themes and symbols of their communitas—music, sex, love, drugs, antiauthoritarianism, antiwar sentiments, pronature, proenvironmental protection, and so forth. These symbols aroused emotions so widely shared and so deeply felt that they obscured the schisms and antagonisms which developed when some participants favored the political goals while others were not willing to relinquish their cultural styles.

Confronted with the need to act together, these young people very often found themselves paralyzed. Their ideology was explicit in not permitting them to favor one aspect of the Revolution over the other, and the result was that they were able to proceed only with haphazard joint ventures, the kind that allowed them to act or at least appear to be acting spontaneously. That their individual desires should occasionally coincide with those of their fellows was fortunate, but this, they insisted, should not be mistaken for organization or structure.

The same dilemma has been observable in many other youth groups with many differing purposes, in some of which the counterculture ideology was attenuated and only modestly developed. The same paralysis of action occurred over and over, for example, in a professional fraternity which was attempting to institute more regular meetings, in a commune which had to find a way to get rid of its crashers (drop-in visitors who stayed too long), and among members of a Jesus cult proselytizing on campus. Communes had collapsed, rock concerts had fallen into chaos, peace marches and religious revivals had fizzled over and over in recent years, in part at least because of this ideology, which dictated that no one must act other than impulsively, globally, and wholeheartedly.

When push came to shove, cultural goals won out over political; it is, after all, easier to "do your own thing" than change a social structure. But for the Woodstock group this was not a satisfactory solution and gave rise to pervasive disillusionment and perplexity. Generally speaking, none of those in the group with which I was acquainted were willing to acknowledge the source of failure of their many enterprises as the need for some structural base. Communitas was to be a full-time, and exclusive, way of life. It was through communitas that a better world was to be constructed; the old ways (structure) had been tried and found wanting, and to lapse into them was to lose everything.

Ecstasy in Everyday Life: Accommodations

Life in the counterculture continued, and various styles of accommodation to an ideology based on ecstasy and accident were developed. Individual enterprises were carried on, enterprises that were tedious, and hardly at all in accord with spontaneous desires. Dishes were washed, dogs and babies were fed, planes and buses were caught, term papers were written. These feats were accomplished in various ways, four of which are by way of: tripping out, flip-flopping, the circuit, and the commune.

One young man, adroit at tripping out, explained that he didn't really mind doing the dishes. Dishes could be "a trip." He could "turn on" to all the nuances, fine points, sensual and emotional experiences of the bubbles, the warm water, the slippery plates, losing himself in the process until it swelled with possibilities and filled his world. He could "blow his mind on the dishes," with or without drugs, but he could not do this in concert with anyone else. It was *his* trip, and it was a private affair. He could spend an evening listening to music with a friend in the same spirit. But he could not carry a heavy piece of furniture or clean a whole house, because for these activities he needed help and that meant coordination of his and someone else's trip, which just didn't work.

Other individuals mentioned different ways of incorporating ecstasy into everyday life. An enterprising fellow described his life as a series of "flip-flops," his phrase for moving back and forth between communitas and structure, making the contrast between the two as sharp as possible. (It gave his life a schizoid flavor, viewed from the outside.) He carried his "straight wig" in his pocket and put it on at times of structure or when he was likely to encounter trouble. Driving on the freeway, appearing in court, going to the bank, meeting his girl friend's family were occasions when he would stuff his abundant, wirey mop into a cap of false, obedient, orderly locks and change his facial expression, posture, and vocabulary to conform with the image. This was more than a disguise, and it was meant to go beyond alterations of mere appearance. He also wore his wig in situations where the people involved knew what he looked like and knew that he had long hair. He donned it when he had to "think straight"; for example, when taking exams he would wear his wig to remind himself to employ the "budget-programming-planning-system mentality." It was the adoption of a social personality, and a setting aside of "his real self," for instrumental purposes. By labeling the switch so dramatically, he knew at all times what was "real" and what was "phoney," and he could keep the boundaries between them exceedingly sharp. Structure never entered his life unbidden or took him unaware. He used it when he needed it, like a quasi-domesticated, evil genie, but he knew it was dangerous. Structure was the enemy, polluting to the pure parts of his life, the counterculture parts, a necessary evil to be kept located and in check at all times.

A third form of accommodation to the collapse of the Woodstock Nation was a kind of regular circuit made periodically by a number of the students when pressures built up in their ordinary lives. They would take off suddenly, alone or in groups of two and three, departing with a minimum of funds, clothing, and provisions, and cluster at freeway on-ramps holding hand-lettered signs indicating their destination. In actuality, their destination was not a place but a condition, that of communitas, and wherever they found it or expected to find it, there they lingered. It could occur anywhere, with anyone, and it was necessary to remain open and alert to this possibility at all times. Some events, places, and people were more promising than others, but communitas, they had learned, could not be scheduled, no matter how good the drugs, the music, the setting.

Yet the diminishing likelihood of finding communitas did not deter them from seeking it and, when they found it, seizing upon it as if it would never return. And one was likely to find the real people with whom communitas was still possible at the onramp of the freeway system. There, they knew, were the other seekers after the lost Eden; onramps were way stations for pilgrims trying to retrieve the memory of the ever-receding ecstasy of earlier days. The impact of their original discovery of communitas had been lasting and profound, a truly apocalyptic transformational experience which had left a permanent mark. And though the freeway onramp was infinitely less satisfactory and shorter-lived than Woodstock, it was better than relinquishing the vision entirely. The young people who had chosen this mode of adapting to the loss of the Woodstock communitas still spent most of their time in the life of structure—working, going to school, enacting everyday routines (often aimlessly), until, overwhelmed by the old memories, they bolted. Their peregrinations were usually confined to weekends, holidays, and vacations, allowing them to resume their regular routines resigned, yet revived, in their belief in the existence of a better way of life "out there."

Yet a fourth form of adaptation was that chosen by a small but very influential minority which called itself "the communards," or "the hard-core ideologues." These people were living in communes and devoting themselves to a full-time pursuit of communitas. They were grappling with the problems of impending routinization of this ecstasy and with the difficulties already mentioned of organizing and carrying out collective actions. For them, every moment not spent in pursuit of communitas was a waste, "a cop out." A number of them had "made it" in the sense of having established relatively stable and enduring communes, with harmonious relations and economic viability. Personally, they had managed to arrange considerable free time for themselves, and socially there was minimal hierarchy and organization. But these accomplishments were secondary to their ultimate goal: reaching the "mind-blowing" state of communitas, of utter unity and oneness on a full-time basis, and, as a result, becoming, "new men." Communitas was conceived of as "passing through the tunnel," and this passage was divided into several distinct sequences. Some communards were agreed to be further along in the passage than others, and it was the duty of the more advanced to help the others come as far and as fast as they could. Transitions were noted with much physical contact and nonverbal communication; few words were necessary or desirable.[13] "Glad to see you here," or "It's nice to see you

[13] This avoidance, almost abhorrence, of labeling and discussing communitas is probably connected to the public nature of language and the inevitable diminution of the subjectivity and privacy of unspoken experiences. Another possible explanation is that labeling defines and fixes that which it refers to; it makes it a part of structure, removes it from the category of flow which is characteristic of liminal states and communitas. Images of what Watts (1963) would call "goo" were prominent in the conversation of the people with whom I was working: transition, amorphousness, continuity, and transformation are central allusions and figures of speech in this culture.

Additional reasons for minimizing the importance of language may be suggested. Communitas requires a conviction of complete sharing. Precise description of one's most ecstatic moments makes it clear that, to some extent, all those involved are having different experiences and are in separate places. The communications about these matters must be imprecise in order for each to assume that he is sharing a trip or vision with another or, at least, that his ecstatic moment is similar to that of his fellows-in-communitas. More than minimal signification of this is intrusive. Thus the Huichols will not discuss their peyote visions, and hippies often limit their descriptions of their trips to comments such as "Oh wow." They are inarticulate from choice, not from inability to describe their experiences. As in the case of symbols, ambiguity is absolutely necessary in order to allow individuals to project their private, most intense emotions and meanings into that which is referred

moving along," were the kinds of comments that signified public recognition of these momentous transitions.

Naturally, not everyone was "in the tunnel," and this was a clear and significant distinction. People who were in the tunnel were completely separate from those who were not, regardless of how far along they had come. "You're in the flow, or you're not," one member said. And this ultimately meant full commitment to the vision.[14]

---

to. Though they are shared, symbols have multiple referents, and ambiguity is essential for their operations.

Similarly, avoiding too much clarity and precision in language has the effect of minimizing the possibility of confrontation of unacceptable ideas and interpersonal conflicts. Disputes cannot develop without recognition of clearly antagonistic interests. In Wirikuta, disputes can be avoided or at least minimized because of the enormous influence and leadership of the *mara'akame*. No less important is the fact that the Huichols do not stay in Wirikuta too long, and many latent issues between people can be postponed until their return. Furthermore, they have taken the most solemn pledge to be of one heart and to share a state of complete accord; without this the *mara'akame* is powerless to protect them, and it is dangerous to undertake the journey at all. In Woodstock, such pledges are not given. Instead, formlessness, permissiveness about and respect for other people's trips, relativism, and looseness of style all contribute to minimizing the possibility of encounters and disputes. Again, imprecise and minimal use of language, like avoidance practices in critical kinship relations, maintains equilibrium; in default of interaction, each can conceptualize matters as he wishes with little chance of encountering evidence to correct or contradict his interpretation.

[14] The same distinction appears repeatedly in Tom Wolfe's description (1968) of a group touring the country on a bus, searching for communitas. In Wolfe's case, the bus is the symbol of total commitment to the quest. ("You're on the bus or you're off the bus.") This is, in part, a boundary-maintaining device, emphasizing the fact of group membership, but it goes beyond that and serves to indicate an elite status. Those who are "in" or "aboard" are "special," set apart, in touch with something beyond ordinary experience. There is no escaping the implication here of a sacred sect.

Briefly, the stages in the tunnel were: the first and most primitive, to "cut through the crap." This consisted of giving up prior modes of existence, learning to share material possessions, relinquishing the desire for privacy, and giving up "being cool," the calculated presentation of self. This stage varied in duration, since people had different backgrounds to which they were attached with varying firmness. This break with the socialization of one's past was for many their only accomplishment, and they never went on to the next stage which involved a fuller sharing with others. "Getting into other people's heads" was the task of this level. It was beyond politics, issues, and interests.

Next came learning to be simple, humble, naked, directly in touch with one's body, in touch with one's fellows, and in tune with nature. New culture forms were needed here—new art forms, poetry, and music, and many regarded this as the most important task of going through the tunnel.[15]

[15] Many of these new art forms were already being practiced, and in them certain themes and characteristics were evident. One of the most striking characteristics was the interest in surrealism, manifested as a delight in paradox, contradiction, and oxymoron. The view of the world as entirely haphazard and planless, lacking fundamental order and purpose, was endemic and anxiety provoking. One way of coping with this distressing interpretation was to affirm the complete arbitrariness of "reality." The relativism resulting from this view was seen as only absurd in the existential sense, and was ridiculous and amusing. Flamboyance, juxtaposition of wildly improbable items or events, and appreciation of the bizarre became ways of controlling chaos by claiming it to be a choice: one was no longer impotent in the face of madness, but beyond it instead.

Some enjoyed their weird juxtapositions for stimulation value alone, mere kicks. But others in the group sought new patterns in the unexpected combinations. Finding sense where none was intended and madness where great order was intended could lead to "wisdom." Through intuition, often aided by drugs, the counterculture people

Finally, the last stage, the millennium, was to occur, bringing with it the development—biological, cultural, psychological—of a new man. At this level man would merge with the cosmos and ultimately lose himself. One pattern would prevail, and complete harmony would be revealed.[16]

This vision was heavily flavored with a febrile, desperate quality, and was often preceded or followed by indications that there might not be a future, that the world could end momentarily, and a drastic alteration in man's nature would be essential if this were to be averted. The sense of doom was ubiquitous, and a view of man's past as soiled and his future as a probable disaster was no cliché; it was a passion and a conviction. The result was that these people felt that if they

could suspend orderly, rational thinking that inhibited the recognition of anything new—in accidents and coincidence—and unsuspected patterns and relationships could be identified. It is the pattern of the dream: unloosed associations freely at play—baroque, grotesque, far-out—but never without inner connections. The great challenge, then, was to overcome appearance and habit, and find that beneath any incongruity "all is one." This is not basically different from the Huichol finding the old man in the little child, or the sun to be really the same as the moon. But among these young people the major thrust was to find insanity in a world which claimed to be sane, to find sanity in places the world usually regarded as insane and, ultimately, to find that sanity and insanity are one.

[16] The yearning and hope in our own society that there may be an overall pattern are not paralleled in a small, well-integrated society like those studied by most anthropologists. There, it is an everyday reality. In discussing the difference between our own society and "the primitive world" in terms of symbolic meanings, Douglas (1966:85) makes the following comment: "Our behavior also carries symbolic meaning. The real difference is that we do not bring forward from one context to the next the same set of ever more powerful symbols: our experience is fragmented. Our rituals create a lot of little subworlds, unrelated. The rituals (in primitive groups) create one single, symbolically consistent universe."

were going to dare even to contemplate the future they would have to come up with something entirely new, outrageous, unthinkable, or it would be worthless and doomed to failure.

Here is the way one informant put it:

The problem isn't simply that there is a population explosion. We could handle more people if that's all there was to it. We have to learn to live together in the future in a new way. More nonverbal communication, without fear of intimacy, the lack of this is what makes us feel crowded and need so much space. . . . It's more than learning to live communally. We've got to learn to fall into each other's being. It won't be easy, and drugs may or may not help. It's that man has got to give up his rationality. He has to become divorced from his presently individualist sharing—not only his bread, his women, his things, but his head, his trips. In fact the idea of everybody has to become part of the process, part of the same trip.

The symbol of this new man and his wholeness was the hologram, where each part reflects its place in the whole. Life itself, in other words, is symbolized by the common cellular structure of life: "It's all mirrored in you." The communards in particular considered the possibility that this new being might not be recognizable when he emerged, but they were convinced that new senses eventually could be developed to identify him, like the senses needed to detect a form of extra-terrestrial life:

It's always present but we can't always identify it. It hasn't yet come into existence. But for sure our present biological species is on the way out and a new biological emergence has to occur for us to get into being all one.

"Being all one," the desire to lose the self within the cosmos, to retrieve the pre-Creation condition of unity, is the ultimate purpose of the Wirikuta quest of the Huichols, and of countless religious traditions in the Orient and Occident. Discovering that the world's chaos is illusory, that underlying it is a stable, single, simple pattern, that the duality and separations which have marked man's life since the First Times—these are basic, widespread ancient religious concerns. It comes as no surprise to find the same concerns appearing here. Nor is it surprising, therefore, that these young visionaries were so profoundly affected by and drawn to communitas.

The communards have accommodated to the intermittency of communitas but at great personal and social cost.[17] To be less than entirely true to the vision loses a communard his standing with his fellows; he is a "cop out," and like a failed shaman is always subject to suspicion. Having the vision requires one to traverse the entire path in its pursuit. Or, like the noncommunard hippies mentioned earlier, one can find the present life of structure sullied and diluted by recollections of the delights of communitas and, lacking the dedication and strength to do more than attempt a shallow fleeting recovery, become the pilgrim of the freeway onramp. This state of affairs is often so demoralizing that the freeway pilgrim is unable to continue either his ordinary life or the wholehearted pursuit of communitas. He drops out.

---

[17] Hippies, of course, are not the only people in our society seeking communitas. The same pursuit can be seen in the proliferation of psychological growth centers, marathons, and group-encounter sessions, underground religious services, experimental "living theater" productions, and so forth.

Such efforts may be construed as constituting an approach toward a more balanced view of human life than that which has prevailed in this society until now. The American concern with efficiency, individualism, and rationality, the impersonal and bureaucratic arrangements of so much of our institutional life, the distrust of extremes in general have all contributed to our rigid limitation of the possibility of ecstasy to a few special roles and individuals.

In contrast, the Huichol is able to relinquish his vision of paradise in the certain anticipation of recovering it. He dwells in primordial unity for a moment and then, reluctantly but rapidly, lets it go. He can re-enter real life and leave ecstasy behind, in its place. For the Woodstock pilgrim then these are the possibilities: copping out, dropping out, or letting go of the Edenic quest as a way of life. As a group, the hippies have not yet learned to do the latter. It is entirely possible for men to learn to integrate communitas into everyday life: ecstasy can coexist with structure. But as the Huichol case demonstrates, such an integration cannot occur without social support in the form of mythological, ritual, and symbolic elaboration, or of competent spiritual leadership and an ideological acceptance of the limited place of communitas within ordinary life.

Wirikuta, Woodstock, and the Freeway Onramp: The Dangers of Communitas

Wirikuta, Woodstock, and the freeway onramp represent, each in its own way, different versions of a religious pilgrimage, an attempt to return to the paradisial state of communitas and to retrieve the primordial unity which in mythical times was man's state. Yet how different are these refugees from Eden. The Huichols proceed to Wirikuta in a quest which in all likelihood will be successful, and will enliven all that the rest of the year may hold. The stability of the already orderly, well-functioning society is thereby enhanced, its poverty and hardships lightened, its mundane levels elevated and rendered aesthetic, its moral postulates transformed into individual choice instead of onerous, impersonal, externally generated and enforced regulation. Wirikuta unites humans with each other, with nature and the supernatural, and with history, and at the same time serves a most necessary symbolic function, the unification of the ideological with the sensory, the instrumental with the expressive dimension, and, like all good rituals, leaves behind a sense of rightness and completion. The social structure is vivified and buttressed at the same time that the individual is most closely allied with its forms and purposes.

What do we see as a result of Woodstock and its sad replacement, the freeway onramp? Here is a form of social upheaval. Its effects are to weaken the society in which it occurs because numbers of people are publicly revoking their commitment to it in the most flamboyant derisive tones. Here, communitas is being sought as a *replacement* for social structure instead of as a part of it. It becomes an end in itself and constitutes what may be considered a genuine threat to order (by virtue of substantial numbers of its citizens withdrawing their attribution of legitimacy to the social order). The disruptive effects of communitas on society in the Woodstock case are paralleled by the disruption it causes in the lives of the individuals who pursue it. These pilgrims are not ennobled but made more cynical as a result of their quest.

But communitas is dangerous beyond its potential threat to social stability. The Huichol pilgrims concentrate on the personal dangers of communitas, and in the trip to Wirikuta the great danger is that they will be tempted to remain there, losing their individual integrity and mortality, permanently dwelling in the womblike past. The counterculture people are far less wary of this peril. Their reluctance to go in and out of Woodstock, their pursuit and conceptualization of it as a viable, permanent way of life is a hazard which for the most part they do not recognize.

Other risks are more evident to them. Apart from the

physical discomfort, damaged health, and narrowed future choices (which are prices that most are aware of and willing to pay), the hippies concentrate on external dangers, in the form of social repression, and the threat of social and cultural extermination. Unlike the Huichol, the hippie is an exile in his own society, and his way of life arouses a passionate and often brutal rejection on the part of the established order. Contacts between hippie and square are often considered polluting and contaminating *sui generis* to both parties. Each one is self-righteous and claims his external state manifests his ultimate goodness and moral superiority. The hippie flaunts his poverty and freedom as symbolic of his contact with a loftier realm. The straight cites his worldly success as a mark of his fidelity to duty and order. Each sees the other as unholy, as a distorted version of what man is meant to be, an incomplete human. The straight—the square —has the forces of repression on his side, and the threat he offers is a relatively simple one. The hippie offers a more complex threat. He is dangerous because he has traveled to uncharted realms, through drugs, sexual experimentations, casual living arrangements, and so forth. And as Douglas points out, "the man who comes back from these inaccessible regions brings with him a power not available to those who have stayed in control of themselves and society" (1966:115). The hippie travels into nonform, into chaos, which is the antithesis of society. As such he is a source of disorder, seen as a filthy, dangerous, and profoundly disturbing influence.

Yet the ultimate danger of communitas is not its capacity to disturb the social order within which it occurs. (I refer here to the danger which makes it alive and ecstatic, and finally unknowable.) The source of its danger is men clinging together in the state of roleless wonder that prevailed in the First Times.[18] Rolelessness is formlessness and nakedness, where people abandon themselves to each other without any boundaries, to be at each other's mercy in acute uncertainty. This venture into chaos, outside of society and self, can never be made safe. Man in the realm of the gods, the animals, the dead, and the spirits dares not ask for maps and procedures. This is the perilous passage back to Beginnings where one can hope to overcome human loneliness and separateness, but may also risk losing his soul and never returning at all. The danger, then, is not that of being alone, but of not being at all. Communitas, retrieved in a well-integrated society like that of the Huichol, is merely an attenuated human version of what men once knew when they were gods and what they may expect in the millennium. But it is powerful enough, in this form, to be the time for which one lives. In view of its unspeakable rewards and its awesome dangers, it is no wonder that entrances and exits are so well guarded by ritual specialists trained intensively to care for those who are ready to go there and who can be controlled and recalled when appropriate. To paraphrase Turner, communitas may be compared to a radioactive isotope in a metal container: it must not be crushed and extinguished; it must be left active and dangerous; when it cannot escape its boundaries at all, it is like a declawed lion. Communitas is thrilling and ecstatic only when untrammeled enough to be genuinely capable of carrying us away.

To envy the Huichol's way to communitas is at once fatuous and irresistible. Undoubtedly, they pay a price for it. It is

[18] Riv-Ellen Prell-Foldes is responsible for bringing to my attention the terror of role suspension inherent in communitas (Personal communication, Los Angeles, 1971).

likely that their access to Wirikuta is one of the most reward-
ing features of their culture and helps them sustain their
poverty, their exploitation, and their ravaged living conditions, but it must also be conjectured that without this great
source of meaning and comfort, they might be moved to re-
dress some of the worse grievances in their present lives.

It can hardly be said that the Huichol are wiser or more
mature than we are because they can re-enter and leave Eden
and we cannot. They have maintained this practice much
longer than we have, and have lived longer with a balance
between organization and ecstasy. Clearly, however, that their
lives are richer and more whole by not excluding one of these
poles at the cost of the others is beyond doubt.

The trick is always in the balance. Communitas may become bounded and rigid, a kind of totalitarianism of the
sacred, as Turner points out, and this happens in monastic
orders, nudist camps, communes, and religious sects, where
the chosen way is guarded too diligently from the philistines
at the gate. Structure is then instituted from within, growing
more strident in its demands for conformity to the supremacy
of the group life. Thus communitas "becomes what it be-
holds" and is engulfed by internally originating structure.
The "group mind" absorbs the individual, and once more
duty replaces freedom. Communitas has now come full circle
and is its own opposite, social structure. Turner concludes:

If one may dare to venture a personal evaluation of such matters,
one might say that much of the misery of the world has been due
to the "principled" activities of fantasies of *both* persuasions. On
the one hand, one finds a structural and ultimately bureaucratic
"ubermensch" who would like to array the whole world of lesser
men in terms of hierarchy and regimentation in a "New Order,"
and on the other, the puritanical levelers who would abolish all

idiosyncratic differences between man and man . . . and set up an ethical tyranny that would allow scant scope for compassion and forgiveness. Yet since both modalities are indispensable for human social continuity, neither can exist for long without the other. Indeed, if structure is maximized to full rigidity, it invites the nemesis of either violent revolution or uncreative apathy, while if communitas is maximized, it becomes in a short while its dark shadow, totalitarianism, from the need to suppress and repress in its members all tendencies to develop structural interdependences.

The problem, evidently, is one of equilibrium. But it is a paradox to speak of balance in ecstasy. The ability to embrace these contrarieties without neutralizing them—to hold oneself quivering between the opposing pull—this is indeed the challenge.

REFERENCES

Bell, Daniel, and Irving Kristol. 1968. Confrontation: The Student Rebellion and the Universities. New York: Basic Books.

Campbell, Joseph. 1970. The Masks of God: Oriental Mythology. New York: Viking Press.

Corey, Douglas Q., and Jeannette P. Maas. 1971. Existential Bible. Unpublished manuscript.

Douglas, Mary. 1966. Purity and Danger: An Analysis of Concepts of Pollution and Taboo. London: Penguin Books.

Eliade, Mircea. 1954. The Myth of Eternal Return. New York: Bollingen.

——. 1962. The Two and the One. New York: Harper Torchbooks.

Furst, Peter T., and Barbara G. Myerhoff. 1966. Myth as History: The Jimson Weed Cycle of the Huichols of Mexico. Anthropologica 17:3–39.

Graves, Robert, and Raphael Patai. 1966. Hebrew Myths: The Book of Genesis. New York: McGraw-Hill.

Guillamont, A., *et al.* (translators). 1959. The Gospel According to Thomas. New York: Harper Bros.

Hoffman, Abbie. 1969. The Woodstock Nation. New York: Random House.

Jung, C. G. 1946. Collected Works. New York: Bollingen.

Lévi-Strauss, Claude. 1966. The Savage Mind. Chicago: University of Chicago Press.

Myerhoff, Barbara G. 1970. The Deer-Maize-Peyote Symbol Complex Among the Huichol Indians of Mexico. Anthropological Quarterly 43(2):64–78.

——. 1971. The Revolution as a Trip: Symbol and Paradox. The Annals of the American Academy of Political and Social Science 395:105–116.

——. 1974. Peyote Hunt: The Sacred Journey of the Huichol Indians. Ithaca and London: Cornell University Press.

——. 1976. Return to Wirikuta: Rituals of Reversals and Continuity. *In* Barbara Babcock-Abrahams, Studies of Symbolic Inversion. Ithaca and London: Cornell University Press.

Neumann, Erich. 1954. The Origins and History of Consciousness. New York: Bollingen.

Turner, Victor. 1969. The Ritual Process: Structure and Anti-Structure. Chicago: Aldine.

——. 1974. Passages, Margins, and Poverty: Religious Symbols of Communitas. In Dramas, Fields, and Metaphors: Symbolic Action in Human Society. Ithaca and London: Cornell University Press.

Watts, Alan W. 1963. The Two Hands of God: Myths of Polarity. New York: Collier Books.

Wolfe, Tom. 1968. The Electric Kool-Aid Acid Test. New York: Bantam.

CHAPTER 2

Symbol and Festival in the French Student Uprising (May–June 1968)

SHERRY ROXANNE TURKLE

Social protest movements in America and Europe have lately taken the form of festivals or carnivals which celebrate the cultural creativity of participants who search, not for the vision of a new political order, but simply for themselves, in a "permanent cultural vibration." As a Sorbonne slogan of May 1968 proclaimed: "Any revolution that demands that one sacrifice oneself for it is just one of your father's revolutions."[1] These groups never aim, it seems, to implement a program, but to express the self instead, or the spontaneity of a new-formed group, freeing themselves by their protest from structural roles and necessities.

Political sociology, confronted by these developments, has turned the study of the phenomena into something of an obsession. The proliferation of literature has been immense, but it has not yet found a conceptual framework that can deal with the utopian, libertarian, spontaneous nature of the protests as anything but signs of a regressive phenomena, a psychodrama, or a vaguely defined cultural expressionism known

---

[1] This, and all other slogans, graffiti, and citations from the 1968 *journaux muraux* are drawn either from personal observations or from a collection of citations edited by Julien Besançon (1968).

as "cultural revolution." Victor Turner (1974:269) has commented that "a major stumbling block in the development of social and anthropological theory has been the almost total identification of the social with the social structural. . . . This has created enormous difficulties with regard to many problems, such as social change, the sociology of religion, and role theory, to name but a few. It has also led to the view that all that is not social structural is psychological."

This is the context in which I describe the place of festival, symbol, and drama in the French *événements* of May and June 1968, to show that liminal, antistructural phenomena are a necessary element in social processes and can be suggestive in understanding the nature of the events.

My argument is developed in three sections: first, in a description of the place of sociologists and sociology in contemporary France, along with a brief description of French sociologists' attempts to deal with the event; second, in a discussion of French social and economic organization which suggests why (a) the bureaucratic structure of French society, (b) the insecure nature of the French political community, and (c) the period of transition in which France now finds herself make France a rich field for an analysis that emphasizes the social need for antistructural phenomena; and third, in a discussion of how the richness in symbols, spontaneity, and dramatic forms of expression of these events can help us understand them as significant political and social phenomena.

The explosion which shook France in May and June 1968 brought to the surface a latent intellectual crisis both related to and inseparable from social and political conflicts in French society. Traditionally, French intellectuals have been very active participants in political affairs. From the Dreyfus affair with a model set by Zola, through the Algerian crisis with dialogue on rebels and revolutionaries by Sartre and Camus, the intervention of intellectuals in political life followed a traditional pattern and involved the greatest writers and philosophers. With 1962 and the coming of peace under Gaullism, France began a period of profound change that was mirrored in a new intellectual climate. Certain sociologists began to play a larger role in the working of the new society as experts and consultants, while others took a greater part in the criticism of that society. To a large extent this second group assumed roles that had once been played by the traditional literary intellectuals of both Right and Left. The intellectuals of the Right ceded their place, it would seem, in political affairs to a school of liberal sociologists with a functionalist methodology. Members of this group, greatly influenced by the work of Weber and the impact of American sociology are committed to a modernized and "rationalized" France, and her response to the much talked-about "American challenge." Like their colleagues on the other side of the Atlantic, French sociologists of the liberal school speak of the end of ideology and of the development of an industrial society with no significant class divisions.

Again, the literary intellectuals of the Left seem also to have been largely supplanted in their roles by social scientists. The *sociologues de gauche* are involved in a sometimes chaotic search for definitions of class relationships in rapidly changing French society.

The surface tranquility of France in the 1960's hid underlying tensions which exploded in the events of May and June 1968. Out of a protest in the Department of Sociology at the University of Paris at Nanterre grew a social movement which struck at every level of French society. It produced a general strike in which workers rejected governmental accords signed by their union leadership, and created a vacuum of power which made it appear for several days that the control of the state could be taken by any group with sufficient organization and will.

Confronted by the event, and then by the disappearance of almost all traces of the event, French intellectuals responded in their traditional manner: they took political stands and began to write. Over a thousand books have appeared about *les événements;* participants recount stories of publishing contracts signed on the barricades. In the debate on the May-June crisis, the traditional literary intellectuals, the men of letters and philosophers, did not play their customary role. Instead, it was the sociologists who were intensely involved in the outbreak and in the debate that followed.

The gamut of hypotheses put forward by sociologists confronting this revolution stretched from the minimal one (taken by conservatives and liberals, that the outbreak was a crisis of *retard et blocage* of the French system and not the result of its development) to what may be called the maximal position (taken by libertarian Marxists, that the crisis was the preparatory irruption for the coming revolution and a response to the incurable malaise of this same system).

Neither the functionalist, structurally minded, nor the Marxist, sociologists had a way of dealing adequately with the fantasy quality of the 1968 revolt. The functionalist position, represented by such sociologists as Raymond Aron, Jesse Pitts, and Michel Crozier,[2] could condone the disruption only insofar as students can be regarded a marginal group turned

---

[2] The positions of three sociologists, representative of the functionalist school, are best expressed in their books and articles appearing after the May days. See, for example Raymond Aron (1968); Michel Crozier (decembre 1968); Jesse R. Pitts (août-septembre 1968).

in Weberian terms more toward ultimate ends than toward an ethic of responsibility. Looked at this way, student radicalism can be condoned as a phase in the life cycle, a pardoned transgression, not to be taken seriously as a responsible political statement. As French society adopts an American-style meritocratic system, the functionalists argue that anxieties are created which become intolerable to French youth who are used to a greater degree of protection provided by more clearly defined expectations. The young people, therefore, try to reduce their tensions by forming a countermeritocracy, a "delinquent peer-group" organization which defines itself by its rejection of the prevailing bureaucracy. The causes for the rejection of the bureaucratic system are seen as emotional; the students drawn to the countermeritocracy are those with high intelligence, yet "with a character that will not permit them to succeed in the adult world" (Pitts, 1968:94). For them, student status may be the highest status achievable, and so they try to prolong it as long as possible. The movement, an organization for assurance against failure, is dangerous because of its negation of rule, order, status, and law. It creates precedents which leave the door open to fascism. The festival aspect of the movement is thus seen as negative, obsessional, and regressive.

The functionalists tend to rely on an interpretation of the radicals' emotional states as a key to their actions. Appraisals of the student leaders as hysterical is then turned (by a dubious logic) into a proof of their irresponsibility and of the psychologically rather than politically induced nature of the May events. The theories of personality which are used in these analyses are poorly elaborated; they are in general drawn from the work of Le Bon, particularly *La Psychologie des foules*, or from Freud's analysis of group action in *Group*

Psychology and the Analysis of the Ego. Both of these theorists emphasize the individual's abdication of his critical faculties and inhibitions in the group: man becomes inconsistent, emotional, similar to the primitive, the child, or a hypnotized subject. Clearly, neither theoretical perspective is conducive to a sympathetic understanding of group festival as a new form of political statement.

Raymond Aron (1968:frontispiece), the most eminent sociologist of this functionalist group, begins his analysis of the event with a citation from Proudhon, writing in February 1848: *"On a fait une révolution sans idée. La nation française est une nation de comédiens."* The quotation sets the tone for Aron's analysis of the festival which effectively reduces the event to psychodrama. The anarchism of the festival, the will to antistructure, he says, is incompatible with the structural demands of modern society. Society, for Aron, is necessarily bureaucratic society. The reaction of the May movement against this political reality is a kind of "waking dream," an illusion with a deadly potential to destroy.

An opposite means of approaching the event is to analyze the movement in relation to the development of historical conflicts growing out of class antagonisms. For the sociologists who write in this second, this Marxist tradition, class conflict and social movements are considered the central motors of social life and not symptoms of dysfunction or pathology.[3]

---

[3] The Marxist positions fall into three groups: (a) The economist Marxists (usually associated with the Communist Party) including C. Prévolst, M. Simon, P. Boccara, P. Juquin, J. M. Bourdet, and L. Perceval. Their work on the May crisis is found in *La Nouvelle Critique,* numéro spécial (juin 1968), and no. 16 (septembre 1968), and in *Economie et politique,* nos. 168–169 (juillet-août 1968); (b) The "political-sociologist Marxists," whose position is represented by J. Colombel (août-octobre 1968), and by André Glucksmann (1968);

The Marxists begin with the study of social conflict and see values and a particular conception of rationality as historical products of this conflict. The need for change is not reduced to the need to correct internal distortions in an established system, but rather is seen in terms of ruptures in an imposed system of domination. In these analyses, the consciousness of the social actor is considered as a social fact and not as a psychological key to the sense of his action.

Regarding the symbolic, dramatic, and festival aspects of the event, the Marxists are more appreciative than the liberal functionalist school. Their willingness to say kind words about symbols, spontaneity, and festivity come less, however, from an appreciation of the form and style of the revolt than from the wish to see in the May outbreak at least the preparatory stage of a social revolution.

The Marxist sociologist who made the most sincere attempt to come to terms with the elements of festival and spontaneity in May was Henri Lefebvre, former member of the French Communist Party, and professor at the University of Strasbourg before coming to Nanterre's Department of Sociology in October 1965. His work at Strasbourg had been on the need to transform radically *la vie quotidienne*—daily life—in modern France. His work on the commune of Paris was highly influential in the development of the situationist movement, whose members made up much of the core of *les enragés* in May 1968. The situationist ideology resonates with Lefebvre's major themes: the importance of *le quotidien*, spontaneity, and the spirit of festival to any revolutionary

---

and (c) the neo-Marxists, a group whose position on the events of May is illustrated by Edgar Morin in "La Commune étudiante," and "Une Révolution sans visage (1968), and by Henri Lefebvre (1968).

movement. Lenin, Lefebvre had said, unduly belittled these matters in the course of his debate with Rosa Luxembourg. For Lenin, the revolutionary movement required an explicit connection between praxis and theory, between class instincts and conceptual knowledge, and spontaneity was far too subjective an element in a given situation. Lefebvre claims to have reopened the debate by insisting that it is an objective factor in itself, and that when theory fails to take advantage of emergent spontaneity it misses an opportunity to offer revolutionary direction. He promises to analyze the role of the rebirth of festival and of spontaneity in revolution. His promise, unfortunately, remains unfilled, since his discussion of spontaneity is thorough only where it is descriptive; that is, he documents the spontaneous nature of the movement and points out that without it there would have been no event. He analyzes the unleashing of spontaneity in terms of the superimposition of three layers of interlocking structures in modern society (precapitalist, industrial, and urban), a superimposition which strains to the breaking point the contradictions inherent in the three. This is very interesting, if not very new, in Marxist sociology, yet it illuminates spontaneity very little.

If the functionalists were obsessed with structure, the Marxists cannot abandon their concentration on infrastructure. Neither group has an elaborated theoretical perspective for dealing with antistructure: why it occurs, the nature of the symbolism it generates, an appreciation of its creative functions, or a realistic way of dealing with its ritualized aspects. For the functionalists, the use of the term "symbolic" becomes a derogatory means of relegating the event to the realm of psychodrama and ritualized madness where it operates in a sphere outside of history. For the Marxists, symbol and festival are equally threatening: a proper revolution can be against the domination of one oppressive structure, but not against all structure. In the final analysis, both the Right and the Left were unwilling to consider seriously the elements of myth, ritual, festival, and fantasy that confronted them in the May action. In the social theory elaborated on both sides of the barricades there seemed to be an unwillingness to consider the essence of the phenomenon, coupled with an unwillingness to consider sociology's profound involvement in the current crisis in French society. It is in response to this refusal of contemporary French social theory to deal with the realities, that I offer the following reflections.

In *The Bureaucratic Phenomenon*, Michel Crozier (1964) presents the thesis that bureaucratic forms of organization exist as cultural patterns in every sphere of French life. This phenomenon was brilliantly described by Tocqueville in *The Old Regime and The French Revolution*. There Tocqueville clearly underscored the relationships between the isolation of individuals and the lack of collective spirit in France as well as the bureaucratic system of French social and political life which placed different strata in a perennial fight for rank and status. Initiative might have emerged only if groups which cut across ranks had developed, those informal associations which Tocqueville so wistfully admired in the American nation, and which he saw as prerequisites for the development of democracy. In France, such development was discouraged by the municipal administrations and by the fiscal policy of the royal administration which preferred an inert citizenry.

Many of the characteristics and qualities of life under the old regime are gone, but the same patterns of individual isolation, strata isolation, and limited communication between groups, have persisted in French society.

In France, informal activities usually take the pattern of

"delinquent communities," organized against a third party.[4] The solidarity of these associations is negative; the groups are unstable and last only as long as there is an external threat. A typical French model of collective activity is a group in which each member carves out a sphere of autonomy, a space where he can express the creativity denied to him in the bureaucratic structure.

The bureaucratic organization of society makes it possible for the French to achieve many of their demands; it provides theoretical equality, avoids conflict and face to face relationships, and at the same time furnishes the absolute authority necessary for action. Within a bureaucratic structure, an absolutist conception of authority may prevail, and direct dependence relationships may be eliminated. At the same time, the members of a bureaucratically organized society can satisfy their need for personal autonomy by operating within a pattern of restriction which has set boundaries: one always obeys the rules but need not submit to another man's whims.

Deeply rooted in French life are the values that condition the prevailing bureaucratic patterns. These include harmony, security, and independence, and contribute to the difficulty of dealing with personal conflict, and the difficulty of taking action in ambiguous, potentially disruptive situations. Like players in a stalemate situation, the members of a bureaucratically organized society wait for an opening, and when it arises (most often in the form of a threat externally imposed), they move, pounce even, and, since change will be accepted only from the top, create a new stalemate.[5]

[4] This term was created by Jesse Pitts. For a discussion of this form of association see his article "Continuity and Change in Bourgeoise France" in Stanley Hoffmann *et al.* (1964).

[5] For a discussion of bureaucratic patterns of change in French society and political life see Crozier (1964) and Hoffmann (1964).

Bureaucratic patterns in France exist in nearly every area of life. The educational system is, for example, bureaucratic in organization and impersonal in pedagogy, creating a wide gap between student and teacher, a gap which prepares the student for the strata isolation of the bureaucratic system elsewhere. Education is bureaucratic in content; what is taught is abstract and totally divorced from actual requirements. The aim is actually to select people for definite social strata rather than train them for productive functions.

French socialization stresses the acceptance of status roles and hierarchies. A French child is forced to accept a sharply defined framework as the inevitable structure which man has projected upon the chaos of living that life is a compartmentalized system of social relationships.[6] Children early learn to accept and deal with a dual reality, just as they learn to live with a dual system of political legitimation and a dual system of routine and crisis in the functioning of their social institutions.

For the French there is an official reality of manmade rules, but this level of daily existence is "only a facade covering a deeper, more mysterious reality which may be felt by the individual in moments of introspection or revealed by art or religion" (Wylie, 1965:295). Hatred for the self in a bureaucratic society is habitually turned to hatred for *les autres*, for those who insist on status definitions and role conformity. A second means of escape from the loneliness of a compartmentalized and isolated life is in the social sphere, through participation in a collective celebration which forges a community with others who are outside of one's formal group. Again and again, the main comment heard from Frenchmen

---

[6] On the issue of socialization see Lawrence Wylie (1965).

about May and June was "that everybody talked to every-body else." The appropriation of speech and language and its revitalization in a new unstructured social context was a way to escape from the compartments in which French discourse is habitually confined.

Thus, the strains of the structured society create the need for an assertion of the total man—which could only be made possible in a celebration of antistructure. A second factor which created this need in French society is the diffuseness of the French political identity. (To be sure, the French feel secure about their civilization, their history, their race. Every French textbook on the primary levels has a frontispiece in which Frenchmen of the past, from the Gauls, through Charlemagne, the medieval and modern kings, the Bonapartes, the great leaders of the republican governments, and General de Gaulle are pictured holding hands in a great chain whose final member is *le petit français*, the little student to whom the book presumably belongs. Frenchmen identify with the mystique of *la civilisation française*.) Despite the sense of security fostered in education, the French do not have a very clear sense of their political identity.

The fact is that since the eighteenth-century revolution, the French people have lived a somewhat schizophrenic existence in which each life has been divided into a pair of alternating identities.[7] French political systems have alternated between bureaucratic attempts at representative governments by assembly (whose substructures were based on patterns established during the monarchy and formalized under Napoleon I), and authoritarian regimes in which one man and one myth ruled France. Such figures (the Bonapartes or de

[7] For a discussion of the French political community, see Stanley Hoffmann *et al.* (1964).

Gaulle for example) are the embodiment of France as a whole, containing in their persons the mystique of the land and of French civilization, the fundamental unity of the French as a race. The pendulum swings from the revolution to Napoleon, from the restoration and revolution of 1848 to Louis Napoleon, from the Empire yielding to the representative government of the Third Republic falling before Marechal Petain, and from the bureaucratically oriented government by assembly of the Fourth Republic falling to yet another authoritarian, General de Gaulle.

This schizophrenia reflects the uncertainty of the French polity as to the bases of its rulers' political legitimacy. On the one hand, popular suffrage leading to the election of representatives to the National Assembly seems to be the basis for the formation of a legal government. Yet in a period of crisis, the ineffectualness of government by assembly, and the feeling that representative democracy corresponds to the particular interests of regional groups rather than to the true spirit of all France, leads to the search for a figure that will unite the nation, for a man who will express, not the individualistic impulses that motivate men at the ballot box, but rather the Rousseauian *volonté de tout*, a will that corresponds not to the sum of individual preferences of voters, but to a mysterious essence of *la belle France*.

The basis of the savior's power has been the assent of the nation to his embodiment as a unifying myth. During a bureaucratized period of government by assembly, political language is that of intransigence and discord, and of a lingering nostalgia for a fundamental unity which can only be achieved at the level of feelings, dreams, and the prospect of a mythical incarnation. During the savior regimes on the other hand, there is the plea for the greater representation of regional and particular interests. Thus no French government is really entirely legitimate, because the bases of legitimacy have never been clearly agreed upon and the political community remains insecure. The periodic French re-enactments of its great political events, the Revolution, the Commune, and so on, may be seen as attempts to return to the now mythical sources of the French political identity and to assert its reality through its symbols.

A third conditioning factor behind the outbreak of May 1968 is that France is now undergoing a period of profound change. French bourgeois society, which achieved in itself the synthesis of aristocratic, peasant, and bourgeois capitalist values, has been falling apart under the impact of increased modernization and Americanization. The old system, synthesized by the bourgeoisie during the Third Republic was something of a functioning stalemate.[8] The much-discussed interwar lag of the French economy which extended into the postwar period, and which was only dissolved with the introduction of American pressure for new managerial techniques as well as American dollars, was not due to a lack of material resources, but rather to the behavior of businessmen in a social system that did not reward innovation but which penalized it instead. French aristocratic values and an emphasis on the family firm created a type of business structure whose chief aim was the social success of important families and not industrial expansion or the making of profits.

In the traditional "stalemate society," each group in France (the peasants, the small entrepreneurs, the regional associations of the provinces, etc.) acted in accordance with the

---

[8] Stanley Hoffmann describes this synthesis in terms of a "stalemate society." For a discussion of how it operates, see *In Search of France.*

bureaucratic analogy and formed pressure groups to keep its acquired rights. The concept of *droits acquis* is central to an understanding of the French social mentality. At any suggestion of a threat, an organization is formed calling for the "Association for the Defense of the Rights of the. . . ." The new sweep of rationalism, beginning with the First Plan at the end of World War II, but only fully implemented with the coming of de Gaulle in 1958, has made profound changes in this state of affairs. The family business is giving way to new industries on the American corporate model, and the percentage of the population in agriculture has been dramatically reduced, as has the number of people living in small French villages—some of which may now have to be artifically maintained for tourists. A managerial revolution has led to the emergence of a new class of technocrats and technicians; attitudes toward credit are changing; the family is less closed and no longer plays its formerly exclusive role in the social life of the child. The Gaullist party, UNR, is intent on creating a French political life, *à l'américain*, free from the ideological debate on nineteenth-century issues that characterized, until recently, French electoral politics.

France is therefore in a period of transition in her social, economic, political, and intellectual life. In this sense, she resembles other societies which, during liminal historical periods, have faced convulsions of millenarianism. Turner's study of these societies indicates that the generation of symbols during their liminal period is suggestive for understanding the ritual, symbolic, and dramatic elements of the May days.

Three aspects of French social and political reality thus suggest the ways in which a society may integrate the liminal period of antistructure into its ongoing processes.

First there is the highly bureaucratized nature of French society and its *horreur de face-à-face*,[9] which calls forth its antithesis, an antistructural movement permitting the development of a more encompassing mode of human relations. Different societies deal with this need for change in various ways, either through regular ritual purgations of structure or, in the the case of modern societies, though millenarianism or social protest movements.

Second, there is the insecurity of the French polity which results in the need to generate and/or share the common symbols and collective dramas that reassert the identity of the French political community.

And third, there is the fact that France is undergoing a phase of transition which might be termed a liminal period in French society.

These conditioning factors make it highly unlikely that the festive and symbolic nature of the May event was a regression or digression into the realm of the "nonserious." Rather it can be seen as the means for positively working out societal necessities. As Turner (1974:268) observes: Yet since the social modalities of both structure and communitas are "indispensable for human social continuity, neither can exist for long without the other. Indeed, if structure is maximized to full rigidity, it invites the nemesis of either violent revolution or uncreative apathy. . . ."

And now let us turn to the social and political meanings of the May festival of life, whose features resemble phenomena associated with liminality, to examine its existential quality, its

[9] "L'horreur de face à face" is Michel Crozier's term. For a full discussion of its genesis and its implications, see *The Bureaucratic Phenomenon.*

vision of politics as theater, its elements of historical ritual, and its use of symbols.

In the liminal period the model of society is that of an undifferentiated whole whose units are total human beings. This ideal is opposed to a differentiated, structured system whose units are statuses and roles. In the structured model, the individual wears a mask which identifies the place he occupies in the social and political hierarchy. In the liminal model, men relate to each other as total persons, as free and equal comrades. To quote Turner (1974:241–242) again, "Life as a series and structures of status incumbencies inhibits the full utilization of human capacities. . . ." The relationships of men in a communitas situation (which may have been generated out of a liminal period—a time out of structure) have existential qualities which Marx has referred to as "the powers that slumber within men." The whole man is involved in relationships with other whole men, and there is a creation of Bergson's "open morality," an expression of change, an *élan vital* or life force. Such relationships tend to generate symbols and new cultural forms. The May events, for example, brought forth a wealth of art, poetry, graffiti, and talk. Through this explosion of words, *la prise de la parole* of those formerly silent, there was a confrontation of men unparalleled in French life. Men talked and worked together in their fear and their exaltation. The events of May created a community where people were, in Buber's terms, "no longer being side-by-side (above and below), but with one another of a multitude of persons. And this multitude, though it moves towards one goal, yet experiences everywhere a turning to, a dynamic facing of, the others, a flowing from I to Thou. Community is where community happens" (Turner, 1969:127). It happened on the streets of France in 1968.

Frenchmen refused predefined social roles, as they refused the division of their political actions from their daily life: "*Toute séparation est contre-révolutionnaire,*" as one inscription put it. And René Viénet (1968:136) commented:

The festival finally gave true vacations to those who had never known anything but work days and days off from work. The hierarchical pyramid melted like a sugarcake in the May sun. People spoke to each other, understood each other "*à demi-mot.*" There was no longer a division between intellectuals and workers, but rather there were only revolutionaries in dialogue all over. . . . In this context the word "comrade" took its authentic meaning, truly marking the end of status separations. . . . The streets belonged to those who unpaved them. The suddenly rediscovered daily life became the center of all possible conquests. The people who worked in the now-occupied offices declared that they could no longer live as before, not even a little better than before. . . . The measure time of capitalism stopped. Without the train, without the metro, without the car, without work, the strikers were able to regain the time that they had so sadly lost in factories, on the highway, in front of T.V. One strolled, talked, one learned to live.

On the walls of the Sorbonne appeared a quote from Mikhail Bakouning: "Revolution is a festival. . . . I see everyone. . . . I talk to everyone." For the first time since the Commune, exclaimed one student, "the reality of the individual man absorbed the artificiality of the abstract citizen." And the slogans and graffiti of May support his sentiments: "*La Révolution doit se faire dans les hommes avant de se réaliser dans les choses*"; "*Ouvrez les fenêtres de votre coeur*"; "*Tout ce qui est réel porte en soi la réalité d'un autre*"; "*Nous ne voulons pas l'homme au service des structures. Nous voulons l'homme"; "Plus je fais la révolution, plus j'ai envie de faire l'amour"; "Il n'y a pas de mortel, de temporel, de limite et d'exclusif dans l'homme que dans les organisations et dans les structures"; "Je vous aime"; "Regardez-vous, vous êtes tristes."*

In May, *"l'imagination au pouvoir."* Imagination, like existential community, is a category in political phenomena little discussed or understood. For the Romantics, the praise of imagination was coupled with a protest against the fragmentation of man. Rousseau disliked the artificial, loved the spontaneous and the natural. The graffiti of May were often quotes from his Arcadian reveries where he accused society of destroying man's inner unity. Whole classes of human beings, the Romantic philosophers complained, develop only a part of their capacities, and in their writings the philosophers expressed the urge for totality through community, a realm in which men could be truly human.[10]

The Romantic critique of society opened up two possible paths. The first was to shun politics and glorify art; the second was to make politics itself artistic, to create it as a new art form, a field for self-expression, for "engagement" and passion. Typical of the Romantics who took this second path was Lamartine who entered politics to transform it into art, and Schliermacher who said: "I love the French Revolution." Several students were to scribble this on the walls of Nanterre in 1968.

When politics becomes a form of art, the role of imagination becomes an essential part of ideology. The artistry of May was the creation of a liberating ritual within which free-

---

[10] For an interesting discussion of the political implications of Romantic thought, see Judith Shklar (1969).

dom, imagination, and fantasy could develop. The role of imagination here is akin to the role of utopian thinking in political thought. It provides the images by which existing structures can be cracked open and re-created. So rigidly organized is the French bureaucratic reality that this creation of images needed to be translated from thought to action to achieve power.

In *Eros and Civilization*, Herbert Marcuse (1955:130) speculates on the functions of imagination and fantasy in politics, basing some of his ideas on Freud's metapsychology which in his words "restores imagination to its rights." Fantasy has its own truth value "which corresponds to an experience of its own—namely, the surmounting of antagonistic human reality." The "knowledge" of the partisans of the ongoing structure which is directed toward finding the means to make the present system work better is challenged by the "knowledge" of antistructure. The latter relies on the play of imagination and the richness of utopian thought: "The truth value of imagination relates not only to the past but also to the future: the forms of freedom and happiness which it invokes claim to deliver the historical *reality*. In its refusal to accept as final the limitations imposed upon freedom and happiness by the reality principle, in its refusal to forget what *can be*, lies the critical function of phantasy" (Marcuse, 1955:136). It is akin to Schiller's play impulse, whose goal is freedom, whose quest is for the solution to a political problem, namely, how to liberate man from an inhuman existential condition.

The May slogans insisted that everyone take his desires for reality—if not for the reality of the present, then for the reality of the future. "*Sous les pavés, la plage,*" affirmed a scrawl on a Sorbonne wall. Statistics, and political science can tell one what is, but as one student quoted from the Surrealist

Manifesto, "only imagination can tell me what can be." Once again, let us look to the slogans and graffiti of May, this time as they underscore the importance of imagination, play, and creativity: *"Le rêve est réalité"*; *"Je joue"*; *"Inventez les nouvelles perversions sexuelles"*; *"L'action ne doit pas être une réaction mais une création"*; *"Jouissez ici et maintenant"*; *Imagination n'est pas don mais par excellence objet de conquête. A. Breton"*; *"Soyez réalistes. Demandez l'impossible"*; *"Oubliez tout ce que vous avez appris. Commencez par rêver"*; *"A bas le réalisme socialiste. Vive le surréalisme"*; *"Creativité, spontanéité, vie"*; *"Je jouis dans les pavés."*

The politics of imagination is theatrical, poetic. It insists on the participation of everyone: *"La poésie est dans la rue."* The theatre of politics likens itself to Artaud's theatre in which magic, violence, and above all the participation of the spectator make theatre an alembic of creativity. Participation was the key slogan of the May days: *"Etre libre en 1968, c'est de participer."* According to the students, sociology gave way to "sociological action," of the kind which looks for truth in participation and experience on the terrain of history. As R. D. Laing has said: "We do not need theories so much as the experience that is the source of the theory" (Roszak, 1969:49). The May participants were unwilling to reify doctrines, insisting that *"toute doctrine est périmée"* (all doctrines are outmoded). The nature of the experience must be spontaneous and joyful, in a context where each participant can relate to others and create with others.

In a 1966 poem, "How to Make a March/Spectacle," Allan Ginsberg had asserted that demontrations should no longer be grave, "heavy" affairs. They should be festivals with dancing, celebration, and the participation of all. The theatricality of politics was taken up by Julian Beck's and Judith Malina's

Living Theatre, which had tremendous successes in France in 1967 and 1968 directly preceding and during the event. Beck and Malina's troupe performed in Paris and the provinces, and participated in May in the arts festival at Avignon. Early in 1968, the Living Theatre arrived at Nanterre, performing before the militants there a production of *Paradise Now* in which the leading protagonists of the later uprising, especially Cohn-Bendit, participated with great relish. The impact of the Living Theatre upon the May movement was enormous. Like Beck and Malina, the *enragés* saw themselves as "magic realists," whose politics are theatre just as their theatre is politics. Their aim, like Beck's and Malina's, was "to zap them with boldness, levitate them with joy . . . to make the land and the elites glow with creation." The movement, like each production of *Paradise Now* saw itself as an instruction period or a study by doing it: in order to study the revolution, one makes a revolution. The revolutionary's work is "to set up situations in which one can study revolutionary structure." The Living Theatre became a symbol in May for the living politics of action and spontaneity: *"Vive le Living Theatre"* proclaimed the walls of Nanterre and the Sorbonne.

As the Living Theatre had become transformed, so did structuralism as an intellectual movement turn into a symbol for the oppression. The dynamics of the process by which a research method was transformed into a cultural symbol are very interesting. French intellectual life has for some time been living under a kind of "structuralist terrorism." The structural orientation of Lévi-Strauss was incorporated into the work of thinkers in highly diverse fields: psychology, literature, history, and political theory, creating a constellation of famous names in French intellectual life (Althusser, Foucault, Barthes, Lacan), whose prestige and army of students made up its "defenders of the faith" in French intellectual debate. In fact, for a while, debate on structural method practically ceased.

At Nanterre, however, were united a group of philosophers, psychologists, and theorists whose method was distinctly phenomenological: Dufrenne, Ricoueur, Levinas, and Lefebvre.[11] During the May events, structuralism and phenomenology were used as symbolic standards under which people organized for political action; the students of Ricoueur fought on the barricades for epistemology.

The French overexaggeration of structure in social organization is congruent with dogmatic intellectual structuralist leanings. Because of such congruence, structuralism became a symbol for hated structures in the society. Structuralism avoids study of the person's social context and deals with language as a relationship between syntactical elements, rather than as a system of meanings. Linguistics in this sense provides a metaphor for the workings of the French University, a system functioning only according to its own laws, without consideration of its human subjects, the students. For the structural linguist, the speaker disappears and nothing remains but language "talking to itself." Similarly, the French University is seen as an order sufficient to itself. The cycle of *études supérieures* or university studies was reduced to pure code, a semeiological system totally divorced from its subjects. The official culture traditionally dispensed by the University was no longer simply attacked as a class culture, but also as a language *pour ne pas parler* (a language to avoid communication). From these qualities of the University came its use as a

[11] For a description of Nanterre at the outbreak of the events, see Epistémon (1968).

symbol of the absurd, the *université de non-sens*, the *fortresse d'Ubu*.

As structuralism became a negative symbol, phenomenology became a positive one. For the students, structuralism and phenomenology lie at opposite poles. The latter suspends the movement of consciousness which is habitually turned toward the world at the moment it seizes that which is offered to it as object. Its prime concern is with meaning as it emerges from experience. The subject and his context are taken into account and the meaning will be different, depending upon whether the subject is imagining, perceiving, wishing, remembering, writing, or speaking to someone. Meaning arrives thus at being seized and examined in its "significant specific intentionality." The students made this phenomenological approach into an emblem of their movement. The congruence is apparent: they too sought to suspend the established order to let new relationships of meaning arise among men in society.

The structuralist dogmatism had negated history, and in the May uprising the participants took the rebirth of meaning, the reinvention of language, and the rediscovery of history through phenomenology as the intellectual emblems for their struggle.

Liminal periods, times out of structure, are periods in which cultural symbols are generated, times during which a society speculates on its ultimate values through the fruitful alienation of the total individual from the partial person. This positive alienation results in a total rather than a partial perspective on life in society. In major liminal situations "a society takes cognizance of itself" (Turner, 1974:239–240). During the May days, French society searched for itself through rituals and symbols.

For the French polity, French revolutionary history operates as a sort of *illud tempus*—a prior time—in the form of a constellation of actors and dramas from which collective images of French political life are drawn. These events and actors are the political society's dominant symbols, symbols which have great power, constancy, and consistency of meaning. Turner has likened such dominant symbols to Whitehead's eternal objects, signifying not objects of infinite duration, but objects for whom the category of time does not apply.[12]

The symbols of liminal periods have a Januslike quality, looking back to the historical past from which they were generated, and facing forward into the new situation, while the period itself is characterized by the redeployment of symbols into a modern context: "Rituals are places in the social process where groups become adjusted to internal change and adapted to their external environment. Thus, the ritual symbol becomes a factor in social action, a positive force in an activity field, a dynamic entity" (Turner, 1967:20).

The liminal symbol operates culturally as a mnemonic, a reminder of cosmologies, values, and cultural axioms, whereby a society's knowledge is transmitted from one generation to another. French political symbols, such as the barricades, and red and black flags, became meaningful in a time of social crisis, the Commune of 1871 for example, when they may have had (like the barricades themselves) an instrumental as well as symbolic value. These symbols tend to re-emerge in ritual re-enactments of the original event, which serve to re-enforce a society's identification with its past. We have pointed out how important such rituals are in France. "Under favorable situations a form generated long ago from communitas may almost be miraculously liquified into a living force of

---

[12] Victor W. Turner, personal communication.

communitas again."[13] Or as Durkheim (1965:474) has pointed out: "There is no society which does not feel the need of upholding and reaffirming at regular intervals the collective sentiments and the collective ideas which make up its unity and its personality."

Marx understood the importance of such symbolic affirmations. For example, he did not glorify the Commune (on the contrary, he felt that it was *peu socialiste* and quite confused), but believed it to be a great model for the future. In a similar vein, Engels stated that "even in the classical era of street combats the barricade has an effect that is more moral than material" (Glucksmann, 1968:25).

The French live in the events of their history as the triumphant continuation of the French Revolution. The accession of Napoleon, the Revolution of 1848, the seizure of power by Louis Bonaparte in 1851, the Commune of 1871, are all viewed as re-enactments of the French "monomyth." Each of these events generates new forms of action, new symbols for the future, which in turn are reorganized by the next generation in a kind of modern *bricolage*. The Revolution of 1789 may have been played in Roman dress, but all those following it were enacted according to a script that led from July 14 and the storming of the Bastille, to 9 Thermidor, the death of Robespierre, the Eighteenth Brumaire, and the rise of Napoleon. These dates and the heroes they symbolize have become an essential part of the Frenchman's mode of thinking about all history and, what is more, the way he interprets his contemporary political reality.

In *The Eighteenth Brumaire of Louis Bonaparte*, Marx considers the problem of the dramatic element of revolution-

---

[13] Victor W. Turner, personal communication.

ary phenomena. Revolutions take place as a kind of costume drama; the event becomes a form of dramatic poetry in which the actors spontaneously repeat old roles: "We suffer not only from the living but from the dead . . . *le mort saisit le vif*."[14] Just when men seem to be in the process of revolutionizing themselves and their society, "they anxiously conjure up the sparks of the past to their service and borrow from them names, battle slogans, and costumes" (Rosenberg, 1965:156). Tocqueville had made a similar comment in observing the Revolution of 1848: "The imitation [of 1789 by the revolutionary assembly] was so manifest that it concealed the terrible originality of the facts; I continually had the impression that they were engaged in play acting the French Revolution rather than continuing it" (Arendt, 1965:264). (Tocqueville too was to join the cast of characters whose personae could be assumed by actors in future situations. In 1968 Raymond Aron insisted that he was playing the role of this philosopher.)

Clearly, in a truly revolutionary situation, the masquerade must cease at a certain point, for "the social revolution cannot draw its poetry from the past but only from the future" (Rosenberg, 1965:167).

The May explosion was not in this sense a revolution, since the actors never really escaped from the drama of a ritual re-enactment. Yet we have suggested that the function of the ritual was political, and maintain that there was a need to reassert the identity of the French polity through a reliving of its major political/historical symbols. Nor does the fact that the situation in France seems to have returned to normal

---

[14] Cited in Harold Rosenberg (1965), p. 154. The citation is from the preface to *Capital*.

prove that the event was antipolitical. Sorel understood the efficacy of a myth in revolution, of the need for an ideal vision. Sorel's perspective assumes the interpenetration of history with an ultimate ideal vision, "much as Bergson conceived of the interpenetration of successive instants in the unbroken continuum of time" (Marcus, 1960:222). The myth becomes a crucial historical force, the critical moral and psychological determinant of history as it moves toward its syndicalist-socialist goal.

Just as the Paris Commune of 1871 identified itself with the revolutionaries of 1789, even to the point of adopting the revolutionary calendar for the Commune's magazines, so the 1968 events were a re-enactment of the Paris Commune. In recent years, there has been a renaissance of interest in the Commune, with studies emphasizing its spontaneity and its symbolism. Analyses by Edgar Morin and Henri Lefebvre demonstrate the symbolic re-enactment of the May days, and the explosion is clearly identified with the Commune. In both cases, a spontaneous urban uprising had occurred during a period of undisputed economic success, each aiming to reconquer the urban centers, and each rejecting political functions and social roles. The insurgents of 1871 and 1968 both wished "to become masters of their lives and of history not only in political decisions, but in daily life" (Lefebvre, 1965:389).

The barricades of 1968 had of course lost all instrumentality. They were a symbol of unity with the grandeur of the 1871 uprising: *"La barricade est l'indication le plus sure de l'essor révolutionnaire,"* proclaimed a wall slogan. Other symbolic forms of unity included the red and black flags which appeared spontaneously after the first night of the barricades, the *pavés*, the techniques of threatening with the myth of a general strike, and the use of revolutionary names for magazines. In 1968 *"Vive la Commune"* was scribbled over walls in Paris and in the provinces and was a model for revolution as a form of poetic invention.

Though dominated by the 1871 uprising, various symbols were drawn eclectically from other chapters of revolutionary history. The Carmagnole, revolutionary dance of 1789, found analogue in the Grappignole, named after Grappin, Dean of Nanterre. The anticlericalism of that revolution was resurrected in the words scrawled upon the entrance to the Sorbonne chapel: "Let us disinter and return to the Vatican the remains of Richelieu, man of state and cardinal." The Third Republic's Law of 1881, whose interdiction is inscribed on all French public buildings in the words *Défense d'afficher*, became a symbol of state repression in a context where expression was all. Its message was replaced by *Interdit d'interdire*, imitating the slogans and graffiti of the Chinese Cultural Revolution. The graffiti became a symbol of freedom in the public sphere. Those who doubted their own eloquence or their ability to juggle the symbols of the French revolutionary heritage wrote simply: *"Je n'ai rien à écrire,"* in order to feel at one with the event.

The heroes of anarchist tradition wrote *"Vive Babeuf, Proudhon, Bakounine, St. Just, Bonnot,"* and one enterprising student researched in the Bibliothèque Ste. Geneviève to reproduce on a Sorbonne wall the list of the demands from the Quartier St. Antoine to the 1793 convention.

New symbols were added: the university and its mandarin professors were equated with the rigid system of French economics which keeps young people from rising in education, law, medicine, and business. The car, which joined the *pavé* as the main element in the construction of the barricades, became a symbol of hated bourgeois materialism.

The May days drew from contemporary cultural forms in French life as well, but restructured these forms to give them a new and dramatically opposed meaning. This reorganization is typical of liminal situations. The objects of everyday life take on a new potency when transformed. For example in one "consciousness-raising" comic strip distributed by the situationists, Steve Canyon, a popular character imported from America, raises his fist and shouts that "revolutionary theory as revolutionary praxis must be recognized and lived by the masses." In another, James Bond is pictured fondling three Las Vegas-type show girls while insisting that "the ideological consciousness of society is erected by the class interests of the bourgeoisie as exploiters." The impact was enormous. The spirit of a movement gained its momentum through irreverence, gaiety, and the reversal of normal status positions. In a way it was not very different from Octavio Paz's description of the dynamics of the fiesta in Mexico: "During a fiesta the ranks and stations of life are violated. We poke fun at the army, the state and church. We flagrantly violate the hierarchies of life and pretend for a moment that we live in the free, non-oppressed world of our fantasies" (Cox, 1970:118).

The momentum of the May uprising was broken by a five-minute radio broadcast by General de Gaulle. The message appealed for order, for a return to routine and safety. The French, exhausted, deprived of food, gasoline, trains, and in some cases gas and electricity, retreated. By mid-June, the streets of Paris had been repaved, this time with concrete rather than the traditional, picturesque but potentially dangerous *pavés*. The buildings were washed, the omnipresent posters were stripped away, and the graffiti was sandblasted off the walls. The festival was over, and the streets of Paris were returned to the tourists.

In medieval times there had been a ritual called The Feast of Fools which related men to history and bound them to each other. Modern France has no such ritualized release from her rigid social institutions. The social protest of May 1968 was the vehicle for such an emancipation—a release at once necessary and desirable.

The violation of social hierarchies, the creation of a space in which men can relate to each other as men (and not the players of social roles), are essential to the healthy working of a society. That entity must be viewed in a delicate tension between the need for both structure and antistructure. Only then can we appreciate the social and political statement that explosions such as the *événements* express and understand the politics which attempts to restore poetry to life in modern industrial societies. As Durkheim (1961:475) prophesied: "A day will come when our societies will know again those hours of creative effervescence in the course of which new ideas arise and new formulas are found which serve for a while as a guide to humanity."

REFERENCES

Arendt, Hannah. 1965. On Revolution. New York: Viking Press.

Aron, Raymond. 1968. La Révolution introuvable. Paris: Artheme Fayard.

Besançon, Julien. 1968. Les Murs ont la parole. Paris: Tchou.

Colombel, J. 1968. Contestation et structures. La Pensée, numéro spécial (août-octobre).

Cox, Harvey. 1970. The Feast of Fools. New York: Harper and Row.

Crozier, Michel. 1964. The Bureaucratic Phenomenon. Chicago: University of Chicago Press.

——. 1968. Révolution libérale ou révolte petit-bourgeois. Communications, no. 12 (decembre).

Durkheim, Emile. 1961. The Elementary Forms of the Religious Life. New York: Collier Books. Reprinted, New York: Free Press (1965).

Epistémon. 1968. Ces Idées qui ont ébranle la France. Paris: Artheme Fayard.

Glucksmann, André. 1968. Stratégie et révolution en France, 1968. Paris: Christian Bourgeois.

Hoffmann, Stanley, et al. 1964. In Search of France. New York: Harper and Row.

Lefebvre, Henri. 1965. La Proclamation de la commune. Paris: Gallimard.

——. 1968. L'Irruption de Nanterre au sommet. Paris: Anthropos.

Marcus, John T. 1960. The World Impact of the West: The Mystique and the Sense of Participation in History. In Henry A. Murray. Myth and Mythmaking. Boston: Beacon.

Marcuse, Herbert. 1955. Eros and Civilization. New York: Vintage.

Morin, Edgar. 1968a. La Commune étudiante. In Edgar Morin, Claude Lefort, and Jean March Coudray, eds. La Breche. Paris: Artheme Fayard.

——. 1968b. Une Révolution sans visage. In Edgar Morin, Claude Lefort, and Jean March Coudray, eds. La Breche. Paris: Artheme Fayard.

Pitts, Jesse R. 1964. Continuity and Change in Bourgeois France. In Stanley Hoffmann et al. In Search of France. New York: Harper and Row.

——. 1968. Les Etudiants et la contre-méritocratie. Esprit, Vol. XXXVI, nos. 373-374 (août-septembre).

Rosenberg, Harold. 1965. The Tradition of the New. New York: McGraw Hill.

Roszak, Theodore. 1969. The Making of a Counter-Culture. New York: Doubleday.

Shklar, Judith. 1969. After Utopia. Princeton: Princeton University Press.

Turner, Victor. 1967. The Forest of Symbols. Ithaca: Cornell University Press.

——. 1969. The Ritual Process: Structure and Anti-Structure. Chicago: Aldine.

——. 1974. Passages, Margins, and Poverty: Religious Symbols of Communitas. *In* Dramas, Fields, and Metaphors. Ithaca and London: Cornell University Press.

Viénet, René. 1968. Enragés et situationnistes dans le mouvement des occupations. Paris: Gallimard.

Wylie, Lawrence. 1965. Youth in France and the United States. *In* Erik H. Erikson, ed. The Challenge of Youth. New York: Doubleday.

PART TWO

THE IDEALIZATION
OF TRADITION
AND REGULATION

Introduction to Part Two

Does having a traditional ideology mean that in any situation there is some traditional ideal, principle, or rule that would apply and could serve as a guide to proper behavior? Certainly in many societies traditions of forefathers and ancestors are spoken of in this way. It is as if, like liquid pouring into a vessel, a flow of tradition could fill any situational container. This idea of an all-pervasive tradition is, of course, either a fiction or an illusion, but often a convenient one. It resembles the assumption, often made in law, that the law is there to be found by judges, that it is always there, lying about somewhere, that judges do not make law, but simply find what is applicable out of some infinitely expandable resource to which they have special access.

In the chapter that follows there is a description of the management of a dispute between lineage brothers among the Chagga of Kilimanjaro. The Chagga have a traditional ideology which is certainly rich in matters relating to the transactions of kinsmen. They also are very aware of having experienced a vast amount of social change in the past seventy-five years, and they have many modern ideas. Thus they have a variety of socially acceptable ideological resources to draw upon in the conduct of their affairs. One of their traditional precepts is that the men of a localized patrilineage are or should be a united and harmonious community. When Chagga brothers have a fight, this mundane reality is not allowed to damage the superordinate mythical reality of lineage unity. One way this is achieved is by defining the issue in dispute as one having to do with the defective character or bad situation of particular *individuals*. If such a controversy is not allowed to expand to involve factions, but is instead contained, limited, and narrowed to the persons directly involved, its divisive danger to the community is minimized (on the expanding dispute, see S. F. Moore, "Legal liability and evolutionary interpretation," in M. Gluckman, ed., *The Allocation of Responsibility*, Manchester, 1972). A further reduction of the dangers of group division can be achieved if everyone is mobilized against one of the disputants, who then becomes a unanimously rejected individual. A consensus of this kind may be very invigorating to the social ties of the rejectors, binding them in common responsibility, righteousness, and guilt in their ill-treatment of an erstwhile insider. The way in which such an individual may lose his social identity as an insider over time is made clear in the Chagga case. The identification of losers is doubtless as common a social process as the identification of winners, but it involves quite different ideological rationalizations. In the case of winners, ordinary symbolic demonstrations of unity *include* them. No special explanation is needed. As for losers, they are specifically excluded from such symbolic demonstrations, and their exclusion requires ideological rationalization; there may also be special rituals of exclusion which must be performed.

Some of the same issues reappear in Evens' chapter on the *kibbutz* which "half-expelled" an undesirable member. The *kibbutz* used the occasion of Ketemyeh's marriage to an outsider as an opportunity to engineer his exclusion from their community. As in the Chagga case, it was not two opposed partisan *groups* which faced each other in the end, but the whole community that confronted the maligned individual. In such situations, the matter of power and popularity of the attacked person is very important to the outcome, or rather in this case, power*less*ness and *un*popularity. But it cannot be explicitly admitted that this is so, lest such imply great uncertainties about the moral rules that are supposed to lie behind the social order. Everyone knows that Ketemyeh's personality is a significant element in the controversy, but that cannot be the official rationale. Evens has emphasized the extent to which abnormal individual characteristics, rather than ideologically prescribed social position, may determine the fate of an individual. One may question whether Ketemyeh would have fared any better elsewhere. In another community without the ideological restraints and humane commitments of the kibbutz he might have been even worse off. That is to say, while his abnormalities caused him to be stigmatized, it may well have been the principles of the *kibbutz* community that kept him from being viciously driven out. Elsewhere he might have been truly expelled much earlier, instead of being diplomatically excluded after long debate and discussion and in a conditional way which tried to mask the realities. In this sense Evens' *kibbutz* case may say as much about the force of ideological commitment as about the efficacy of stigma.

For a planned community to design regular procedures with which to deal with dispute is to admit that it is inevitable in community life. The inhabitants of some antiplanned do-your-own-thing communes, being committed to a utopian dream of anarchic individual liberty sometimes have no such means of reaching decisions or of settling disputes. All they can do is walk away from controversy. They may reach an impasse when they have to decide who is to wash the floor, let alone settle a dispute between members. In some of these anarchic communal arrangements members cannot act together on the most trivial of matters. They can cope with disagreement only by ignoring it. To acknowledge it is to recognize the ideologically inadmissible: that in a state of total freedom people do not "naturally" generate total agreement.

The *kibbutzim* and *moshavim*, despite a commitment to utopian community goals, have a far less idealized conception of natural man as an individual, and have little faith in his spontaneous behavior. Thus they have regular procedures with which to arrive at decisions. But in the course of reaching these decisions, they prefer not to acknowledge fully that there can be profound differences of interest in their egalitarian communities. It is ideologically troublesome that even in a state of approximate economic and political equality, their members' interests are not identical, and not everyone is equally likeable.

In Abarbanel's chapter on the distribution of the milk quota in the *moshav*, the specific problem with which the community was faced was entirely new. The milk quota had been imposed by the government from the outside. The new regulation placed two sets of *moshav* members, the dairymen and the vegetable growers, in a position of mutual opposition. The situation was dealt with as one in which venerated general *moshav* principles of internal organization, such as economic egalitarianism, rational planning, and communal harmony, were deemed suitable guides to the particulars of applying this new rule, despite its external provenance. Bargaining, though it took place and was fairly public, could not be discussed explicitly, as it would have implied uncertainty of the outcome and a concomitant element of nonrationality in the rules. Both difference of interest and nonrationality of outcome were ideologically inadmissible circumstances.

The case of the *moshav* raises in a special way two major issues which are not as clearly visible in, but pertain to, all the other chapters. First there is the very obvious fact mentioned earlier (Editors' Introduction to Part One) that all of these communities (or temporary aggregations of persons) are very far from being completely autonomous social units. They are anything but isolated, and are firmly imbedded in larger societies which impinge on them in many ways. Second, some issues are of a kind that do inevitably generate *factional* splits, and these perhaps more than others, must be swept under the ideological rug if any semblance of community harmony is to be maintained. One is struck by the dependence of small social collectivities on the vagaries of their social environment (such as the impact of government regulation on the *moshav*) as well as their helplessness in the face of other matters quite beyond their organizational control, ranging from population explosion (the Chagga) to genetic abnormality (the *kibbutz*). In every case dealt with in the chapters of this book, the communal ideology of the collectivity under discussion is not part of a national ideology. Thus for all of the collectivities discussed here, one ought to consider the possibility that for them one significance of an ideology of communal harmony is as a statement about the integrity of an inside world as against a larger, alien outsider's world. As the earlier chapters indicate, this is explicit in counterculture communities, but such holier-than-thou ideological boundary drawing is evident in many much more conventional groups. The idealization of an absence of internal conflict may be in part a statement about closed ranks in relation to outsiders. It may be a way of representing such closed ranks in a seemingly nonhostile frame, a way of pointing up the existence of a boundary while stressing an inner rather than an outer reference. The availability to such units of expulsion/emigration, or fission/ hiving off/disbanding as an ultimate resort if all else fails, may enable them, for the time of their existence, to maintain not only an ideology of communal harmony, but some degree of actual internal peace. The anarchic communards may *walk away* from any decision of controversy because they cannot cope organizationally or psychologically with such a living refutation of their ideals. The planned or traditional communities, which have procedures for dealing with such matters, *do not walk away* from these problems, but in extreme cases can *send them away* in a physical sense, or such communities can divide or disperse and have regular techniques for doing so. These communities invariably have an expulsion boundary and a capacity for fission; indeed, their awareness that such extreme measures are available may lend hidden force to seemingly calm and temperate discussions.

CHAPTER 3

Selection for Failure in a Small Social Field: Ritual Concord and Fraternal Strife among the Chagga, Kilimanjaro, 1968-1969

SALLY FALK MOORE

The symposium to which this chapter was a contribution, by implication, placed dispute in opposition to an ideology of community harmony, treating them as antithetical when in fact, not being of the same analytic order, they are not contradictory. An ideology is a set of ideas, disputation is a complex of events; consequently, they are not always as directly opposed as they might first seem. For the purposes of a particular occasion, general and rather ambiguous ideas can be used selectively, interpreted or adjusted in such a way as to produce apparent congruence between an ideology and action. This chapter will show the way in which a particular African community deals with internal quarreling and seeks to reconcile its actions with its ideology of community harmony in the midst of ubiquitous dispute. Field data on the Chagga of Mount Kilimanjaro, gathered in 1968–1969, serve as illustrative material.

Three different perspectives on the analysis of dispute and its management will be suggested here. Episodes of dispute and settlement can be regarded: (1) as explicitly recognized ordinary activities of many levels of Chagga social organization; (2) as having ideological, ritual, and symbolic elements (particularly in the settlement process); and (3) as part of the long-term history of competition and collaboration among individuals within a social field.

First, concerning Chagga social organization. There are persons at the household, minimal lineage, lineage, and neighborhood levels as well as persons in the formal administrative system whose culturally prescribed roles explicitly include the settlement of dispute. Furthermore, the fact that settling disputes is one of the recognized functions of designated persons at virtually every level of Chagga organization has implications that go beyond the structural. Chagga arrangements seem to postulate that disputes are a mundane part of social life, a disruption likely to occur that must be provided for in all enduring relationships. The Chagga tend to treat dispute as the result of individual misconduct, and this in itself implies the idea of living in a moral order. In this way they are unlike those utopian thinkers and political ideologists who conceive dispute to be the product of an unjust society, avoidable if social inequities are removed. When Chagga "elders" hear disputes and judge their fellows in informal neighborhood hearings they consider themselves the instruments for enforcement of a moral-legal system that ought to govern behavior in the neighborhood community of which they are a part. But men and women are imperfect, misconduct is common, and depravity may even reach the point of witchcraft—hence disputes. If the difficulties are thus defined as a problem of individual behavior and not as a problem inherent in the social order, there is no serious contradiction between the ideals of communal harmony and the fact of dispute. It is a matter of making certain exceptions.

Second, looking at dispute and settlement from its ideological, ritual, and symbolic aspects, it is seen to be intertwined with social organization. Legal matters deal with practical affairs. They seem to concern empirically discoverable facts. One thinks of judicial procedures as dealing explicitly with defined and real issues in a rational manner. Hence, legal matters are not usually analyzed by anthropologists in terms of the beliefs they involve and their symbolic and ritual manifestations. But there are also always veiled issues, allusive and symbolic references, embodied in the actions which regularly lead to the resolution of disputes. In the Chagga context, the very personnel present at a neighborhood hearing and the things said may be interpreted as symbols of and allusions to the various levels of Chagga community life and its ideology. While a neighborhood hearing deals with a narrowly time-specific episode of dispute, such a proceeding is in many respects a succinct reiteration of long-term social ties, and of theoretically timeless common values.

But there is even more involved. It is not just that the content of a hearing implies the existence of some kind of cultural and social background. The process of hearing and decision can be interpreted as two parts of a *ceremony of social transformation*. Although the importance of rites of passage has long been recognized as a social means of marking the change of status of *individuals, groups, and categories*, there is no comparable concept in anthropology for those rites which transform social *situations*. For example, an election in the United States transforms competition between candidates into the naming of the officeholder. A formal meeting of a corporate body or its representatives may make decisions that will bind its members and transform their previous relationship. Signatures on a contract may alter the obligations of the signing parties. In this secular sense, a judicial (or quasi-judicial) hearing and decision is a ceremony of social and situational transformation. It turns a dispute between two parties into a declaration by a third. The formal process alters the social situation, and it is understood beforehand by all concerned that the process is intended to do so. And like religious rituals, ceremonies of situational transformation are invalid and ineffective if improperly conducted.

The third perspective sees intermittent incidents of dispute as a part of the long-term history of a small group. Like intermittent episodes of cooperation, exchange, and celebration, disputes recur again and again. Dispute, as well as collaboration, has cumulative effects in sorting out the relative positions of individuals. For the Chagga, much of this sorting out occurs within a small social field in which everyone knows everyone else, and where everyone is in some degree socially (and potentially economically) dependent on the others. In such a social setting disputes can be a normal part of the competition between individuals for resources and prestige. The winner of a dispute may not only win on the particular issue of the particular case, but he may simultaneously succeed in permanently scarring the reputation of his opponent. What appear in the short run to be quite discrete incidents may be shown to be connected in the long run. In series they are part of a process of ranking. In the circumstances of Chagga land shortage, they may be part of a desperate elimination contest in which the community must slough off some members to survive. This sloughing-off of a community "brother" must be rationalized and made congruent with the ideology of community solidarity. If a community must reject one of its own and yet extol the values of community and brotherhood and mutual obligation, it must somehow identify the rejected person as a justifiable exception to these common commitments. Rejection of a member must be turned into an affirmation of community. Dispute and its social consequences help to make that possible.

Unofficial Hearing of Dispute: The Chagga Lineage-Neighborhood Nexus

Chagga elders commonly hold informal hearings of dispute in the neighborhoods in which they live. In their quasi-judicial roles these neighbors pronounce decisions on the cases brought by their fellows: they fine people, order specific performance of obligations, and the like. The personnel of these unofficial tribunals vary from case to case. The hearings are held when there is a case to hear, and not on any regular schedule. Only one case is heard on any particular occasion.

The community the elders represent is the very neighborhood of which they are residents. They *are* the community, or rather, they are a part of it. In the decisions they pronounce, they express its order and values, social and ideological. The process of settling particular cases is partly a process of asserting local social control over individuals. The power of the local community to control its own is represented by the extent to which the elders' decisions actually end episodes of dispute. However, to the extent that the decisions fail in this, or fail to end disputes permanently, the failure is evidence of the greater force of other processes simultaneously at work in the neighborhood.

The explicitly empirical and explanatory elements in many judicial processes have received a great deal of scholarly attention. (For example in anthropology, Gluckman, 1955; Fallers, 1969. In law, the list is too long to cite.) The focus has been on the apparently rational activities of those who hear disputes, listen to arguments and witnesses on both sides, expend time sorting out facts, consider relevant moral and legal principles, and ultimately reach a decision. But attention to these refinements of judging should not cause us to overlook the cruder basic transformation of social relationships embodied in the procedure. As a mode of settling disputes the judicial process is, among other things, a regularized, rationalized rite of situational transformation. It changes a dispute into something else. The process of hearing and decision, and the submission of the disputants to the authority of deciders, transforms a disagreement between the parties into an affirmation by others. What started as a dispute becomes a ruling. What was a controversy between disputing individuals becomes a decision pronounced by others. Aubert has said that the legal process transforms dyadic relationships into triadic relationships (1963:16–20). Judicial decisions do even more. By the end of the judicial process the relative positions of the disputing parties are altered in relation to each other, in relation to the tribunal, and in relation to the community the tribunal represents.

In the simplest cases, the affirmation of the hearing judges is partly or wholly congruent with the position of only one of the disputants. The loser no longer has a dispute merely with his original opponent, he has a disagreement with the opponent *and* the body that decided in the opponent's favor. The loser bows, not necessarily to the decision, but to the deciders. If he gives up his original position, it is not because he no longer thinks he is right, but because he knows his claims cannot prevail. *He accepts, not being wrong, but losing.* The transformation of a dispute into an affirmation of power and authority, whereby there is a shifting of action from the disputants to the judgers, is a social ceremony found (with local variations) in societies the world over. Often it is accompanied by explanatory statements referring to commonly held norms and values that are put forward to account for the choice between disputants and to give moral and logical force to the decision. The whole process reaffirms both the actual power of the deciders and the presumed social and moral efficacy and correctness of the norms and values referred to. Thus it reiterates a general commitment to a social and ideological order at the same time that it transforms a specific controversy into a nondispute.

When a dozen Chagga kinsmen and two or three unrelated neighbors assemble at a crossroads clearing between their gardens to hear out, and end, a dispute between two of their number, they are engaged in just such reiteration and transformation. So is a Chagga partriarch when he assembles his minimal lineage branch or "house" to settle a dispute. All are responding to an immediate situation; and their actions are shared partly by the immediate circumstances, their individual experience, their common traditions, and their specific ties to one another, to the disputants, and to the wider community.

The Chagga live in localized patrilineal clusters, the gardens of father and son and nephew and cousin and a score of other agnates all lying next to or close to one another. There are no compact villages but many contiguous farms, each housing one or two nuclear families. At its edges each patrilineal cluster of farms is interdigitated with others since there is a land shortage and little open space. Also at intervals, scattered across the map, there are homesteads of unattached individuals whose agnatic clusters are sometimes elsewhere in the same village, sometimes in another village.

The "farm" is really a homestead garden, the *kihamba*. It is a permanent possession. It produces subsistence foods and a cash crop, coffee. The land is perpetually renewed by manuring, and watered by an irrigation system that draws from the mountain streams. A group of agnatic kin and neighbors, hearing a case, is thus composed of persons who are lifelong associates, and whose fathers were associates, and some of whose offspring will be occupying the same gardens. Being a neighbor is not a transient circumstance, nor is it one without obligation, even for those neighbors who are not kinsmen.

This underlying presumption of the permanence of local residence, that is, the permanence of neighborhood, contributes to its social dominance. Land shortage intensifies this localism, but localized lineages pre-existed current conditions of shortage. Some men move away. But those who remain are the descendants of those who stayed on before them. Today the rural Chagga community in the central belt of Kilimanjaro consists of those who have stayed over several generations. They see themselves as permanently attached to their land and to one another. In urban industrialized societies the possibility of groups disbanding, of members moving away, is in the background of all social relationships. In the rural Chagga neighborhood this is not a serious consideration for most people.

Since a man's legs are the principal means of Chagga transportation, proximity of residence is an important element in the formation of relationships. Educated men with salaried jobs, and shopkeepers and craftsmen (and there are one or two such in most large local lineages) travel to work on buses and have wider-flung networks than do their brothers and cousins who are exclusively farmers. But even these salaried men depend heavily on local agnates and neighbors for many forms of cooperation and social communion. Despite their positions of economic advantage, these educated individuals have additional, rather than alternative, social resources.

Together, kinsmen and neighbors celebrate the great events of life: the christenings, and the marriages and the holidays. Together, they mourn the dead. Together, they do whatever occasional cooperative work each man needs done to keep him going, whether it is working in his maize field at the foot of the mountain, or helping him to build a house. Kinsmen and neighbors act as witnesses when a man allocates land to wife and sons. They watch each other's banana gardens and coffee bushes when the owner is absent. They protect each other together. When one of them surprises a thief, or is attacked and makes an outcry, all neighbors are expected to run to the rescue. There are even times when their presence deters wives left alone in the huts from acts of infidelity while their men are working (or drinking) elsewhere. However, just as well developed as is the ideology of cooperation within each household, within the lineage, and within the neighborhood, and as explicit as are the norms of obligation and cast of characters to whom obligations are owed, just so developed are conventional ways of indicating mistrust, conventional candidates for mistrust, conventional subjects of dispute, and conventional ways of carrying on disputes with the self-same range of persons.

For example, for every proper Chagga marriage, a man is appointed the *mkara*, the person whose duties toward the couple and their families make him a go-between in all matters, including quarrels. Dundas put it this way in 1924, and it is still true: the *mkara* "is agent, best man, instructor, and guardian to the couple throughout their married life; for instance, when husband and wife quarrel it is for him to reconcile them, it is also for him to look after the father-in-law's interests and to see that the husband gives him his due" (Dundas, 1968:232). Expectation of dispute and provision for handling it is thus built into every marriage. Routine behavior in marriage itself sometimes includes conventional expressions of profound mistrust. Some Chagga husbands make a habit of asking their wives to taste their food before they eat to show that it has not been poisoned. Presumably for those who do it regularly this is a mere convention, just as is the Chagga custom that a man who offers another a calabash of beer in the *pombe* shop ought to take the first sip to show that the beer is not poisoned. Thus, in some formal social gestures, the Chagga affirm amity negatively, as a denial of enmity. Evidently in marriage there is no presumption that everything will go smoothly between the affinal groups, nor for the couple themselves. It is of interest that the settlement of quarrels arising from the marriage is one of the tasks of the very person who has had a key role in the positive negotiations and rituals that brought about the marriage in the first place.

Analogously, inside the "house" (a minimal patrilineage three or four generations deep), one of the normal responsibilities of the senior man (the grandfather, father, or senior brother, depending on the configuration of the extended family) is the handling of the disputes that arise between brothers or patrilineal cousins or between their wives. These he often deals with before the assembled kinsmen. Thus disputes are expected and provided for among the very men who are ideologically conceived as the most closely knit group in Chagga society. The house, the most intimate group of agnates, regularly engages in rituals of amity. They celebrate their close relationships in slaughtering feasts in which they drink the slaughtered animal's blood together, eat some of the meat that is cooked at the slaughtering place, and divide the rest according to lineage seniority. Slaughtering is done for the general well-being of the house as well as on special occasions of illness, danger, or misfortune, to ward these off. The slaughtering feast also serves as a ritual re-enactment of everyone's proper place in the house-lineage hierarchy. There are believed to be severe supernatural penalities for any violations of protocol. A villager of Mwika who died with very swollen and cracked lips was said to have died in this manner because he had stolen and eaten the portion of meat that should have been given to his father many years before. Thus the ideology provides supernatural sanctions for violations of the norms of ranking and agnatic obligation. By implication, having such an ideology anticipates just such violations.

For all their cooperation, ritual and economic, the house (minimal lineage group) is almost invariably also riven with bitter rivalries between father and son, between father's brother and nephew, and between brother and brother. Brothers, cousins, sons, and nephews compete for a senior man's favor, for his material wealth (formerly cattle, today usually land), and for their well-being to be mystically maintained by the senior of the house. The competition between brothers does not always erupt in direct expressions of hostility between them. Instead, it sometimes emerges in accusations of witchcraft made by the wife of one brother against the wife of another. These occur when a woman is sterile, or her child is ill, or she herself is not well. These disputes, like those between brothers, are usually heard by the senior man in the house, frequently in the company of other agnates.

More distant agnates and unrelated neighbors also quarrel on occasion, sometimes over boundaries, land tenure, and other matters, and their cases are heard before an assorted group of neighborhood elders. As indicated earlier, the neighborhood is a resource for help in work and other mutual assistance of various kinds. It also constitutes the guest list for all big beer parties to celebrate christenings and marriages, and its members attend the *matanga* (the ceremony for redistribution of a dead person's responsibilities and property) when any one of local importance dies. While slaughtering feasts involve close agnates only, beer parties to celebrate the important events of life always include neighbors and friends as well as a wide range of agnates and affines. Thus there are rituals that are exclusive to agnates, and there are other rituals that involve the company of the larger local community of which the agnates are a part.

It is evident that the neighborhood, the total local lineage cluster (made up of many houses or minimal lineages), the minimal lineage (house), and the individual household, are all units of economic cooperation, and of ritual celebration. They each are also arenas of competition and dispute. Each level of organization is provided with mechanisms for internal settlement of controversy. (For an interesting discussion of the importance of "Legal Levels and Multiplicity of Legal Systems," see Pospisil, 1971:97–126). Disputes arising inside any of these levels of Chagga social organization may be settled within it, or may draw units of higher level into the settlement process before a settlement is reached. Since every Chagga individual belongs to all of these levels of organization, he may try to mobilize a higher level to settle a controversy he is involved in at a lower one if he thinks it will help his cause. One advantage of the neighborhood hearings is that anyone can be brought into them.

An assortment of neighborhood elders may be called upon to hear a marital dispute, to resolve a fight between lineage brothers, or to settle matters between a father and son. Though such disputes might have been settled at a lower level of organization, they frequently are not. *Disputes thus have the capacity to rise*, to originate in one nexus of social relationships and be settled by representatives of a collectivity of a higher level. At whatever level above the lowest a settlement is reached, the transformation of the dispute into a ruling is simultaneously a declaration of the coercive power (such as it is) of the settling social unit over the units of lower order that it encompasses. By transforming the dispute into a ruling, the declaring-judging unit also reaffirms its own social importance.

When closely associated men assemble to settle a dispute, they are reiterating their connections in other social spheres; they are mobilizing the multiplex ties (Gluckman, 1967:19) that connect the neighborhood to force an end to a controversy that divides some of its members. First by assembling, and ultimately by sharing responsibility for the decision, they once again bind themselves to one another. That there is a public dispute at all means that there is bad feeling between two individuals. At present the substantive nature of the controversies that arise among the Chagga is such that they can rarely be resolved through compromise or reconciliation. On the contrary, the ending of the dispute usually means that the loser will be even angrier than he was at the beginning of the fight. The group that decides against him accepts a share of his anger and, with its social weight, forces him, as much as it can, to accept having lost. It often does not altogether succeed in this. But in the attempt to produce a binding decision, it is as if all the positive aspects of the total complex of long-term relationships, all the repeated events that reinforce and validate the ties of kinship—affinity, neighborliness and friendship—were being weighed against a single episode of controversy.

In these Chagga lineage or lineage-neighborhood hearings the substance of the controversies never has to do with community action or collective interests, but invariably concerns encroachments, injuries, and competitive claims between pairs of individuals. In some societies precisely such disputes between individuals become enlarged. Each disputant mobilizes backers. The disputants and their backers confront each other as discrete factions or opposed social segments. Elsewhere I have called this process, "the principle of expanding dispute" (Moore, 1972:67).

But in the rural Chagga neighborhood the disputes between individuals which are adjudicated before a lineage or neighborhood assembly are usually not allowed to expand. They are contained, and confined as much as possible to the individual disputants. Open partisanship is usually limited to members of the immediate family or household of the protagonists. For the containment of dispute, one mechanism well-described in literature is the array of cross-cutting ties that binds the disputants to the hearers and the hearers to each other (see for example, Colson, 1962; Gluckman, 1956; Turner, 1957). But the Chagga material suggests that on Kilimanjaro an additional element is operative: the neighborhood-kinship nexus is not a corporate group.

The community described here, the neighborhood that joins kin and nonkin in permanent physical and social contiguity is in no sense a corporation. Using M. G. Smith's definition of social corporations as a basis for judgment, it fails from the start to meet his criteria of corporateness, in that the neighborhood does not have definite social boundaries (Smith, 1966). The membership of each little neighborhood nexus overlaps other collectivities just like itself. The persons mobilized for any particular neighborhood activity are situationally determined. Membership varies somewhat from occasion to occasion. At its core is what Mayer has called a repeatedly recruited action-set or quasi-group (Mayer, 1966).

The many overlapping kinship neighborhoods own no property. They control no offices. They do not act as a unit in relation to other collective units, but *perform as a unit only in relation to individuals*. They are mobilized by individuals to witness allocations of property, to settle disputes, to provide labor, and to celebrate important occasions. They are an important and permanent economic and social resource for individuals. They are also a significant and continuous part of the machinery of social control. But they are not a corporate organization.

Precisely because the kinship-neighborhood nexus is not a corporate group, *it does not constitute a political arena in which expansion of dispute would be serviceable*. There is no formal organization of minineighborhoods as such, no focus for political competition to which factionalism in dispute might contribute by providing additional grounds for collective division and opposition.

Yet for all the lack of organized corporate unity in the neighborhood, the Chagga continuously need and use the same core of kinsmen and neighbors and affines and friends to see them through the work, the crises, and the celebrations of life. For most purposes the neighborhood is their primary social resource. However, for the purpose of settling disputes, there are alternative paths that can be taken. It is possible to step out of the nexus of lineage and neighborhood and appeal to a whole array of fairly accessible official persons—the TANU hierarchy (the Tanzanian African National Union, the only legal political party in Tanzania), the Village Executive Officer, the pastor (or priest), the Primary Court. All these outside agencies are available to the ordinary man for the settlement of controversies. But, the chances are that he will have to bring in his witnesses from the neighborhood, and also his local reputation, to help his cause. The nexus of lineage-neighborhood thus often retains its primacy even in proceedings involving officials. It is not surprising, therefore, that the local elders should continue to be resorted to as the principal forum of first instance for the hearing of dispute.

In fact, only a relatively small percentage of lineage and neighborhood cases reach any higher level official. Most are heard and re-heard locally, and when the Primary Court or the Pastor or the Village Executive Officer is drawn in, it is as part of the strategy of one of the parties, and the outcome in that tribunal may be no more an ultimate determination, nor a final closure of the controversy, than the other kinds of hearings.

In the past few years, Magistrates of Primary Courts have been assigned to sit in villages other than their own. This is obviously intended to try to provide a more impersonal form of justice, since the Magistrate's network of influence and obligation is in his own village and seldom extends outside it. But this depersonalization of the Primary Court does not necessarily lead to "justice," since the man who can mobilize the most witnesses, and who has the most impressive witnesses, and can make a persuasive argument himself, is likely to win his case. This is particularly so if he is relatively well educated like the Magistrate. Attorneys are not allowed in these Courts, though some people consult "bush lawyers," local men who know their way around the judicial system, in preparing their cases, and occasionally a particularly afflu-ent individual will consult the one African lawyer in the nearest town, Moshi, which is twenty-five miles away.

It is often as difficult in a Chagga case as in an American one to discover what really happened. The ability to mobilize witnesses is directly affected by a man's influence in his neighborhood. In a land-boundary case I heard through from its inception at a neighborhood hearing to its subsequent hear-ing in a Primary Court, witnesses who had agreed to testify for the plaintiff simply did not appear in Court at the ap-pointed time. I knew all the surrounding circumstances, and I know that the defendant was a man of much greater influence in the neighborhood than was his opponent, and that the evening before the Court hearing, he had approached every witness the plaintiff had called or might have called, asking each as a personal favor not to appear, or if they appeared, not to testify to certain damaging admissions he had made in the neighborhood hearings. They acceded to his request and he won his case, just as he had won it in the neighborhood, not on the basis of greater rectitude but on the basis of greater influence, despite the fact that he did not know the Magis-trate, who came from the next village.

It cannot always be so cut-and-dried and predictable, how-ever, or no man who had lost his case in the neighborhood would ever try again in the Primary Court, and a number do. Most, however, do not. Some may be put off by the incon-venience, the fees, the formality, the requirement that Swahili be spoken rather than their own tongue, Kichagga. (Most

Chagga speak Swahili yet find Kichagga more comfortable.) But surely most cases never get to the Primary Court, not only for such reasons, but also because the real arena of life for most men is the neighborhood. It is in the neighborhood that the most important transactions take place, and where the most controversies arise. The neighborhood is where the relationships of opposition and competition are ultimately played out, whether or not outsiders such as the Pastor, the Village Executive Officer, or the Magistrate are drawn in to end some episode along the way.

Decades of Controversy: Unsettled Settlements

The repetitive and continuing quality of rural Chagga social relationships is just as much part of relationships of competition and dispute as it is a part of amity and cooperation. The same individuals fight with each other again and again in separate episodes over the years just as certain pairs and sets of individuals cooperate intermittently again and again over the years. These repetitive disputes are part of a general process in which competitors are sorted out into winners and losers.

The bitterest competitive struggles are between brothers and other agnates for land. A Chagga father customarily provides his elder sons with garden plots to live on when they marry, and keeps his youngest son with him to inherit his house and remaining gardens. (This is the custom, at any rate, in the region of Vunjo.) But a father is under no obligation to give his sons land if they do not behave toward him with proper respect and deference. As the magistrate said of a youngest son who had taken coffee from his father's bushes without permission, "What he should do is to try to please his father so that he may get his land when he dies. And if he fails

to please his father, then his father may give the land to another of his sons, and the defendant (the disobedient son)
may not make any claims, because it is the property of the
father and not his" (Mwika, Primary Court Records, Case
No. 3, 1967). There is no absolute legal right to the father's
land on the part of the son. He may be disinherited for cause.

Nor is there anything that binds a father to treat his sons
equally. Many fathers do not. Traditionally, the eldest son is
for various purposes the principal heir and successor, the
youngest son the next favored, and the middle sons are least
favored (Gutmann, 1926:30, 36; HRAF translation, 22, 27).
This unevenness of paternal allocation may have had less serious effects in earlier times when there was no shortage of
land and the situation of population increase may have been
quite different. Thus fathers have much power over their sons
in real as well as mystical ways, and there is bitter competition among the sons.

The depth of the bitterness of these disputes, and the over-
tones of sorcery and witchcraft that are always in the background are attested to by the statement of the magistrate
(Mwika, Primary Court Records, Case No. 34, 1967) in a
ruling on a dispute between brothers and a nephew over the
ownership of a piece of land. The magistrate, reprimanding
the defendent for not heeding a previous court order, said,
"the action of the defendant could bring about misunderstandings between brothers and it could even cause death." In
another case in the same Court (Mwika, Primary Court Records, Case No. 80, 1967) a son had previously been fined four
tins of beer and a goat by the elders in his neighborhood for
threatening to kill his father during a dispute over land. These
cases could be multiplied many times over. Fights about land
are no casual matter.

Sometimes the rivalry between the men is thus expressed directly in disputes over land and boundaries, or in disputes over generosity in giving beer and meat and the like. But sometimes the rivalry erupts in fights between the wives. It is not surprising that the wives of brothers accuse each other of witchcraft whenever misfortune is manifested by sterility, insanity, serious illness, or death. The competition for a father's favor, and for male offspring, is also indirectly a competition for land.

A man who dies without male issue enriches a kinsman, most often his brother or nephew who inherits from him. Theoretically the plots are considered to be held by individuals alone. However, any man who wishes to sell his land is under obligation to offer it first to his local agnates. They have first refusal. They are likely to covet it for themselves or their sons and may compete with each other to buy it from a less-fortunate kinsman. Consequently, men have a strong contingent interest in the land, debts, and state of health and fertility of their kinsmen. What is a disaster for one is likely to be the good fortune of another.

Hence disputes among agnates and between their spouses could be characterized as endemic. Chagga disputes are as much products of the current configurations of Chagga social organization and economic situation as are the bonds of cooperation forged within it. Individuals are placed in structurally loaded positions of mutual competition from which there is virtually no egress. Any tipping of the balance that favors one competitor or brings misfortune to the other is likely to burst into an episode of hostile action or accusations of witchcraft. Often hostilities are carried on in strategic ways that permit the cooperative and ritual activities binding the lineage together to continue. One of the most common ameliorating devices is to undertake the most aggressive action through substitutes and surrogates; that is, diviners and other outsiders are called in to order hostile action at one remove. Moreover, almost any hostile act can be more or less retracted, for there are ritual ways of asking pardon and of demonstrating reconciliation. Rituals of reconciliation and of acceptance of settlement, often made so much of in the literature, may be nothing so much as evidence of the frequent instability of such settlements. The ritual may in fact signify the social probability of the opposite of what it says, and is very likely a sign of the strong chances of re-eruption of controversy between the same parties rather than a sign of peace achieved. Indeed, the meaning of the emphasis placed on reconciliation as the underlying objective of African judicial procedures ought to be reconsidered in the light of long-term dispute (see Gluckman, 1969:22; 1967:432–434, and Turner, 1957).

What follows below is a description of a long-term antagonism that took place in a Chagga lineage cluster of which I have detailed knowledge. The account demonstrates that the processes that engender competition and dispute can be more vigorous in certain situations than the pressures for settlement, and it shows how these operate. The dispute is currently very much alive. It started twenty years ago when the wife of a youngest son, one of three full brothers, failed to become pregnant in the first four years of her marriage. The wives of the other brothers had several children each. The sterile woman suspected the wife of the middle brother of witchcraft. The eldest brother had a great deal of land and was also very prosperous from a salaried job he held, so his wife was a less suitable candidate for suspicion. The middle brother and his wife were poor and hence might have had more cause to desire the sterility of this woman, particularly since the paternal land might ultimately become their property if she did not have a son. The suspicions of the sterile woman boiled over into rumors. The neighborhood hummed with speculation. The suspected woman was furious. The situation became intolerable. Something had to be done.

The sterile woman virtually had to bring such an accusation after four childless years, lest she be sent home to her father and replaced by another wife. Sterility is a legitimate ground for sending a wife away. A man has a right to expect children from a wife, just as he has the right to certain services from her. Thus the accusation of witchcraft against her sister-in-law must be seen not only as an expression of hostility between the women, but as a preventive measure taken by the sterile woman to forestall a possible divorce. Her sterility had to be the fault of another person lest it be construed to be her own fault. Today Christianity prevents the husband from keeping the sterile wife with him and taking on a second wife for childbearing, a more humane arrangement that was possible in earlier times.

The father of the three young men was sorely pressed by the sterile woman. She and her husband (the youngest son) lived in the patriarch's household, and he eventually decided that some remedial measures had to be undertaken. The patriarch assembled all the people of his minimal lineage who were around at the time, together with their spouses and children. The husband of the accused woman, that is, the middle brother, was temporarily living and working in another district and thus was not among those present when the father assembled the kinsfolk in his homestead to deal with the accusation of witchcraft. (The people there were the father, the mother, two of their three sons, the unmarried fourth son of the father by an inherited widow, the wives of the three married sons, and the children of two of them.) The patriarch slaughtered a black goat and took up a cup of its blood and handed it to each of the three wives in turn. Each had to swear as she drank that if anyone who drank the blood had witchcraft substance, she would die.

A few days later the husband of the suspected woman returned home. He was in a rage as word reached him that his wife had been accused of witchcraft. He stormed over to his father's house and asked why he had abetted such an accusation. The father said that he did not particularly suspect *that* son's wife, but suspected them all, as attested to by his putting them all through the same ordeal. The indignant son was not satisfied; but he felt he could do nothing. Through the ritual ordeal of blood his father had succeeded in ending temporarily an episode of dispute without actually finding anyone guilty.

However, the unhappy, infertile woman went on being childless, and no one died. She must have continued to plague her father-in-law with her complaints and suspicions. Once again recourse was taken to mystical measures since the first try had not worked. A *mganga* (diviner, curer, witch doctor) was sent for from the Pare tribe. The Pare are known among the Chagga for having great powers of witchcraft and effective modes of curing and divining. The church has made life difficult for Chagga *waganga* which may be one reason for importing experts. Another is certainly the advantage of bringing in a neutral outsider who is not himself involved in the dispute.

The *Pare mganga* was called by the father to find the person responsible for the sterility of his daughter-in-law. He appeared at the homestead wearing skins and a strange headdress and bringing with him bones, claws of animals, and a calabash as instruments of his craft. Together the diviner, the father, the sterile woman, and her husband slaughtered a goat in secret. (Examining the intestines of a goat for divinatory purposes is mentioned by Gutmann, 1926; HRAF translation, 612.) They asked the diviner what to do. He told them that the childless woman should go to the house of the suspected sister-in-law when she was away and take all her clothes and burn them. (This is a standard remedy against witches.) The sterile woman waited until a day when her sister-in-law was down in the maize gardens, went to her house, took all her clothes and burned them, just as she had been told.

When the suspected witch came home and found all her clothes destroyed she had a letter sent to her husband asking him to return at once. He came home and decided to employ comparable countermeasures. He in turn called a diviner to discover who had burned his wife's clothes and to take suitable steps against such a person. It must have been fairly plain to all concerned that the sterile woman was responsible. But by leaving it ambiguous and doing conditional witchcraft against whosoever had done the deed, a confession could be forced. The diviner came and took some soil from the doorway and did some magic that would kill the person who had burned the clothes if she did not come forward and confess. Though all this was done "in secret," sufficient publicity was given so that the patriarch heard what was going on. The father told his youngest son's wife that she had better go to the house of her sister-in-law and tell her that she had burned the clothes and ask forgiveness so that her life would be spared. She did so, and the angry accused sister-in-law said that she would forgive her if she brought a goat, and if, furthermore, she paid for the clothing that had been destroyed. The sterile woman sent the goat, and her husband paid for the clothes. But the husband of the accused woman was not satisfied, and he went to his father and said, "I know what you did," alluding to the slaughter of the goat, a custom that was sacrilegious by local Protestant tenets, "and I am going to report you to the pastor." He went to a church elder who was their immediate neighbor (and an affinal kinsman) and told him all about what had been happening in the household of his father. The church elder went to the father's house and demanded an explanation. The father told him his version of the events. The case was duly reported to the pastor, who held a hearing on the father's un-Christian activities. The result was that the father and all those involved, including the suspected witch, were expelled from the congregation for about two months.

Despite the church punishment, no one in the lineage had the slightest doubt but that all these goat slaughterings and hirings of *waganga* were effective. For one thing, two years after this whole affair, the sterile daughter-in-law conceived and bore a child. For another, within a year after these goings on, a married sister of the three brothers died. When the husband of the accused witch heard this he went to his father triumphantly and said, "You thought that my wife was a witch, when you had the witchcraft yourself. You see, your daughter is dead." He meant that his sister had died because of the forces their father had released when he slaughtered the goat.

There have been subsequent disputes that are undoubtedly related to these earlier ones. For example, the patriarch had a serious quarrel with the father of the accused witch. The case was significant enough to be heard before the elders and to be resolved in a rite of reconciliation. The elders decided against the old man who had slain the goat, and fined him in beer. He brewed the beer as he had been ordered to do, and the two fathers drank it in the house of the "guilty" patriarch, in the company of the members of their lineages and such affines and neighbors as had heard the case. Another dispute connected with the first series surfaced in 1964 when the husband of the accused witch was excluded from a series of lineage goat-slaughtering feasts at which his elder brother was host. The father cooperated in this exclusion. The middle brother was excluded on the ground that he had been selling *his* goats and not sharing them with his brothers as he should, that is, that he had been ungenerous in the giving of slaughtering feasts. The excluded brother then gave a slaughtering feast and invited all the men of the minimal lineage except the elder brother who had excluded him. This competitive slaughtering dispute is still going on in the form of new episodes, though moves are being made currently to try to smooth matters over.

To this day, twenty years since the inception of the dispute, the two women involved in the original quarrel do not speak to each other, do not attend beer parties at each other's houses, and do not permit their children to visit each other's houses, nor accept food lest it be poisoned. All this animosity continues despite the fact that the once sterile woman has over the years produced seven children. It is interesting to note, however, that the husbands of the two women have never broken off their relationship. The slaughtering quarrels are between the middle brother and the eldest brother, not between the middle brother and the youngest brother, who have continued to be on speaking terms and to attend slaughtering feasts together. But, it is evident that the position of the middle brother is not a good one. His relations with his father are strained—because he reported his father to the pastor and made accusations of witchcraft. His relations with his elder brother are strained over the alleged lack of generosity in slaughtering, and over a more recent incident in which he obtained a sheep from a friend of his father by claiming he was asking for it on behalf of his father for ritual slaughter, when in fact he sold it soon afterwards. His relations with his younger brother are strained over the old quarrel between their wives, though the two men have made a special effort not to breach any of the formalities of ritual amity. The only brother with whom he is close is the son of the inherited widow, that is, a half-brother whose ritual slaughtering partner he is. No doubt partly because of his dismal prospects within the lineage, his grown son has recently volunteered to emigrate, to join a government land-pioneering scheme distant from Kilimanjaro, far away in Mwese. Thus the repercussions of the quarrels of one generation are felt in the next.

The episodes of dispute form a series. From the start the middle brother had less land than his siblings. His consequent poverty made his wife a suitable suspect of witchcraft in the sterility case. A show of anger against his father after that episode made him breach the norms of respect and permanently impaired their relationships. His lack of resources may have made him ungenerous in slaughtering, but it is evident that his father and senior brother were positively eager to find fault with him and punish him. This provoked him to countermeasures in kind. Doubtless it was also poverty that led him to make misrepresentations about his purpose in buying the sheep, but this angered his senior kinsmen further. The chain of events seems repeatedly to have provoked from the victim the kind of behavior that could justify the way he was dealt with initially. Effect justified cause. None of these episodes can be fully understood by itself. Yet each could appear as a separate case if one were not aware of the series.

Conclusions

On one level the case demonstrates the role of dispute in the process of "selection for failure" in a small social field. It shows how dispute is relevant to the process by which some persons are identified as losers in the long-term competition for scarce resources. In the Chagga context, land is an increasingly scarce resource. As the population continues to expand, the ratio of men to land becomes ever larger, and some men will have to leave. In many places socially desirable land, that is, land within the localized cluster of lineage gardens, is no longer available. Indeed, the point has been reached where there is not really enough land to go around. The lucky few who have salaried jobs can manage with very small garden plots, but the others cannot. Sufficient land to support a farm family can be obtained only by shrinking the number of shares, that is, the number of competitors. The poverty-stricken few are likely to accumulate debts, and eventually some are forced to sell their land to their more prosperous brothers. Seen in its grossest demographic-economic terms, the process is one of selecting particular individuals to leave, and others by implication to remain.

The process of identifying certain people as expendable, as losers, can be exceedingly painful and difficult in the intimacy of the Chagga lineage-neighborhood complex with its ideology of communal solidarity. I suggest that some of the discomfort of rejecting a brother is ameliorated if he can be identified as a bad character who is at least partially to blame for his own plight, as a person who is morally inadequate. I

suggest further that particular traditional structural arrangements predispose certain persons to be suitable candidates
for this classification and rejection. Some of these are: the circumstances of being a middle son; or of being a man whose
father died early in life and who is consequently under the
aegis of an uncle who prefers his own sons; or the misfortune
of being the son of a rejected wife, when there are other sons
of a loved wife. Circumstances such as these place certain
persons more at the mercy of their kinsmen than others, and
make them more likely to be taken advantage of in the competitive manipulation of situations. They have fewer powerful natural supporters than are provided others by the norms
of the system. I would venture further that the fact of being
at a disadvantage, helpless and likely to be cheated, leads to
envy, anger, and ill-will, since most human beings do not have
the saintly capacity to accept blows with equanimity. Whether
a man is in fact envious or not, his poverty may lead the community to suspect him of malice, and consequently he or his
wife may be accused of sorcery or witchcraft when mis-
fortunes befall his more fortunate kinsmen. That would seem
to have been the situation in the case described here. Disputes
are bound to follow, the outcome of which are likely to re-
confirm the relative positions of social strength and weakness
that gave rise to them, as well as to produce more examples of
controlled anger in the loser. He may, in his fury, do as the
victimized middle brother did in this case, accuse his father
openly or even take action against his father. Yet to show
anger against a father or a senior brother is a serious violation
of the norms of lineage seniority, with serious moral and mystical implications. The more incidents there are of displayed
resentment, the more confirmation there is that the victim is
immoral and deserves no better than he got. A poor man is

less likely to be generous in slaughtering than a rich brother. If, as in the case described, the father and brothers want to make something of it, his poverty itself becomes a delinquency in the performance of ritual obligations. In this context, initial unfairness provokes the very behavior in the victim that ultimately justifies and legitimates penalizing him further.

This is not to say that individuals cannot sometimes overcome these handicaps of structural position through attributes of personality and strokes of good luck. Nor is it to say that persons in favored positions cannot lose their advantages through unattractive personality and overreaching behavior or bad luck. In fact, most people are probably lucky enough to be in more ambiguous and less fixed positions of social advantage and disadvantage. What is being argued is simply that among the Chagga today certain traditional structural circumstances favor some and put others at a disadvantage. Under present conditions of extreme shortage of land those circumstances that favor some over others are likely to produce further social and emotional dislocations and disruptions that are likely to continue over the years and accumulate in the same direction.

The role of dispute and of the local settlement of episodes of dispute in this process is evident. I hope it is clear that I am not saying that all disputes among the Chagga are part of such an inevitable cumulative series, but rather that where this kind of progression is seen disputes are a regular part of the sequence.

The relation of these incidents to the ideological background that extols communal harmony is complex. Analyzed on one level, the various Chagga processes of settling dispute may be interpreted as invariably reiterating and confirming the communal harmony aspect of the ideological superstructure, and the solidarity of the commitment of a particular social and ritual community to that harmony. But analyzed in the context of the long-term demographic-economic process of getting some of the men to relinquish their land, the processes of settling dispute can be shown to have quite a different significance.

It is important however, to recognize that the long-term significance is not at issue when a hearing is under way. From the point of view of the elders, what they are doing is instance-by-instance settlement. They are dealing with an incident, an episode. It is, of course, the case that sometimes the long-term history of a relationship is related by the parties during the hearing, and is argued about, but it is presented essentially to illuminate the instance at hand. While the deciders may hope to end the controversy once and for all, their immediate concern is to terminate a particular episode of dispute, not to consider the larger social issues of distribution of resources, population explosion, and the long-term sorting out of social strength and weakness that is taking place in the community, and to which the dispute itself contributes a small tally of scores. Thus the parties and the deciders conduct this ritual of situational transformation, the hearing, to change the immediate situation, not to grapple directly with large-scale matters.

Ritual transformations of social situations imply changes of obligation. These must be accepted by, or imposed on, those involved. In circumstances that make the change of obligation likely to be unacceptable or at least unattractive to one party (or several) those imposing the change are strengthened by the conviction that they are right and that they are imposing obligations on the objecting party legitimately. The repetitive elements of judicial ritual contribute to this sense of correctness and legitimacy, and symbolically tie the particular event to more general ideas and characteristics of social order. Procedural correctness lends validity to substantive action. It gives the sense that things are being done as they should be done.

To maintain a sense of correctness and legitimacy while placing resented obligations on the shoulders of a close kinsman or neighbor, it is necessary to be more than procedurally correct. It is also necessary to have a sense of ideological rectitude. To penalize a member of one's own community, a kinsman, or a fellow neighbor, is to do the very opposite of the giving of assistance that is part of the ideal role of community members. Yet every Chagga neighborhood hearing closes with the allotment of penalties or a decision that displeases one party. Someone loses the case. The norms that idealize community generosity evidently do not apply to those who are construed to have broken local norms. They have, so to speak, disqualified themselves. The onus of penalizing someone is thus partly shifted from those who are actually doing the penalizing (that is, doing the legitimated harm) to the person who has to endure the penalty. In terms of this part of the ideology he is penalized because he is at fault. The same applies to any inequality in the access to resources. It is very much like a penalty and must be justified. Thus the middle brother in the case recorded is not generally perceived by his uterine brothers as persecuted, but rather as a person who is morally suspect.

The common conception and phrase in which a judicial (or quasi-judicial) decision is characterized as "settling a dispute" obviously does not fit too well the durable antagonisms that seethe inside small, permanent, face-to-face communities. The idea that a judicial decision settles a case probably implies a model in which the dispute itself arises out of a single-interest transaction in a situation in which there is no enduring relationship between the parties. Even in industrial societies there are many disputes that do not fit such a model. Certainly most disputes inside the Chagga neighborhood do not. As Gluckman says, after recounting the aftermath of some of the cases he analyzed in *The Judicial Process*,

These brief notes show how unsatisfactory it is, for certain problems, not to trace back the origins of a dispute before the court into the past, and to follow it into the future. Quarrels in groups such as Barotse family villages can rarely be finally settled. Increase in numbers leads to dispute over resources; failure to conceive children or deaths can leave resources plentiful, but largely through fears of witchcraft produce quarrels of another kind. An attempt by the court to give a ruling which hopes to produce harmony cannot in fact eradicate the likelihood that either the old quarrel will be renewed, or new quarrels will arise (1967:433–434).

I have tried to carry the gist of Gluckman's remarks a few steps further by showing how certain disputes in Chagga communities can be interpreted in terms of long-term processes of competition within them and the ways in which these are rationalized. That is, I have turned the question around, and I am arguing that one of the ways to approach the problem of unsettled settlements is to identify the endemic processes of competition and cooperation in a particular community in a particular period of its history, and then to see what place episodes of dispute have in relation to that background. The day may come when most important Chagga disputes are not with kin and neighbors. When and if that day comes, it will not mark the ultimate achievement of Chagga communal harmony, but rather will signify the end of the Chagga lineage-neighborhood-complex as a community.

REFERENCES

Aubert, Wilhelm. 1963. Researches in the Sociology of Law. American Behavioral Scientist 18:16–20.

Bienen, Henry. 1967. Tanzania, Party Transformation and Economic Development. Princeton: Princeton University Press.

Colson, Elizabeth. 1971. The Plateau Tonga of Northern Rhodesia: Social and Religious Studies. Manchester: Manchester University Press.

Dundas, Charles. 1968. Kilimanjaro and Its People. 1st ed., 1924. London: Frank Cass and Co.

Fallers, Lloyd A. 1969. Law Without Precedent. Chicago: University of Chicago Press.

Gluckman, Max. 1956. Custom and Conflict in Africa. Oxford: Basil Blackwell.

——. 1965. Politics, Law and Ritual in Tribal Society. Chicago: Aldine Publishing Company.

——. 1967. The Judicial Process Among the Barotse. 1st ed., 1955. Manchester: Manchester University Press.

——. 1969. Ideas and Procedures in African Customary Law (ed.). London: Oxford University Press for the International African Institute.

Gutmann, Bruno. 1926. Das Recht der Dschagga. Munich: C. H. Beck. English trans. A. M. Nagler. New Haven: Human Relations Area Files, Yale University.

Mayer, Adrian C. 1966. The Significance of Quasi-Groups in the Study of Complex Societies. In Michael Banton, ed. The Social Anthropology of Complex Societies. A.S.A. Monographs, No. 4. London: Tavistock Publications.

Middleton, John. 1960. Lugbara Religion: Ritual and Authority among an East African People. London: Oxford University Press.

Moore, Sally F. 1972. Legal Liability and Evolutionary Interpretation. In Max Gluckman, ed. The Allocation of Responsibility. Manchester: Manchester University Press.

Pospisil, Leopold. 1971. Anthropology of Law, A Comparative Theory. New York: Harper and Row.

Smith, M. G. 1966. A Structural Approach to Comparative Politics. *In* David Easton, ed. Varieties of Political Theory. New Jersey. Prentice-Hall.

Turner, V. W. 1957. Schism and Continuity in an African Society. Manchester: Manchester University Press.

——. 1966. Ritual Aspects of Conflict Control in African Micropolitics. *In* M. J. Swartz, V. W. Turner, and A. Tuden, eds. Political Anthropology. Chicago: Aldine.

Unpublished sources. 1967. Handwritten Primary Court Records. Mwika, Kilimanjaro.

CHAPTER 4

The Dilemma of Economic Competition in an Israeli Moshav[1]

JAY ABARBANEL

Many modern, secular, planned communities have been organized on the assumption that, with rational planning, an egalitarian society could be created which would eliminate what the founders regard as the basic problem in capitalist society: the social inequities and contradictions based upon unequal distribution and unequal control of the means of production. The Israeli *moshav* is one such planned community, and the circumstances surrounding a dispute in one *moshav* will be analyzed in this chapter.[2] A dispute within the community challenges the very tenets on which it was founded, tenets both ideological and organizational. The men who created these communities argued that with careful organization, and equality in access to both the means of production and the manner of distribution, a local egalitarian social unit

[1] This chapter, in an earlier version, was presented as a paper at the annual meeting of the American Anthropological Association in New York City, November, 1971. I wish to thank Max Gluckman, Sally Moore, and Barbara Myerhoff for their valuable comments and suggestions.

[2] This fieldwork was supported by the Bernstein Israeli Trust of the University of Manchester. The research was carried out from 1966–1968.

could be formed which would do away with the basic contradictions that plague capitalist society. Such arrangements were supposed to eliminate the cause of serious, structurally derived disputes. But can a community be designed to avoid major internal conflict? And when a serious dispute arises in a *moshav*, how is it to be reconciled with the rationale of moshav structure?

The founders and planners of these communities assumed that conflict in capitalist society stemmed from competition over economic resources. Were that source of trouble eliminated, they argued, there would be no possibility of fundamental conflict, no disputes based on ideological or organizational contradictions, no splitting and dividing of the community against itself. The ideology did not go so far as to postulate that no disputes at all would exist in the well-planned community, only that after economic competition was eliminated, whatever disputes there were would arise from individual problems and issues, not from inherent social conflicts.

This chapter will show an Israeli *moshav* confronted with some of the very problems which theoretically could not occur and the manner in which these were interpreted and resolved to preserve community social relationships and ideological forms. The ideological background of the *moshav* will be sketched to show why the dispute had to be carried on in an idiom that emphasized a general community of interest that the dispute itself belied. For despite their vigorous ideological and organizational commitment to equality and unity, the farmers in the *moshav* split into different interest groups when confronted with a government milk quota which they were forced to divide among themselves. The controversy which ensued was one in which underlying organizational contradictions became manifest and brought into the open the fact that there were diverse economic interests in the *moshav*, notwith-standing the members' philosophical commitments.

I present one particular situation for analysis rather than deal with generalities from several situations. This is what Gluckman (1961) has called the "extended-case method," and what Van Velsen (1967:129) calls "situational analysis." This method has become more and more popular, because it presents the reader with some of the material from which abstraction and generalizations are developed. Equally, if not more importantly, the case method emphasizes the dynamics of social process in preference to a static structure. Analysis of a dispute helps to bring out differing alignments and inter-ests, thus analyzing behavior in terms of conflicting norms rather than in terms of structural regularities.

The Background

The formal organization of the *moshav* developed from ideological considerations propounded by Zionist socialists who were dedicated to the establishment of a Jewish home-land in Palestine through pioneering. The idea of a "return to the soil," in order to establish the basis of a Jewish national home, combined with the values placed upon agriculture in collective and cooperative settlements, led to the establishment of *kibbutzim*[3] and *moshavim*,[4] farm communities based on the principle that members should have equal access to economic and political resources. The members of these settlements be-

[3] For a description of the kibbutz by the members themselves see Leon (1969) and Weingarten (1955). For sociological analyses see Spiro (1956), Talmon-Garber (1962; 1965), and Talmon-Garber and Cohen (1964).

[4] There is an extensive literature describing and analyzing the *moshav*. See, e.g., Weintraub (1964), Weintraub and Lissak (1964), Weingrod (1966), Shokeid (1971) and Baldwin (1972).

came the pioneers of colonization in Palestine; they established the prevailing norms and values of its Jewish community and dominated the economic and political institutions of Jewish life. Members of kibbutzim and moshavim were thus seen, and saw themselves, as having an elite status within the broader Jewish community (Eisenstadt, 1967:45).

While more numerous than the kibbutz, the moshav is not as well known outside Israel. There is a fundamental difference between the two types of settlements. The moshav is made up of family farms of equal size, with each farm engaged in its own type of agriculture, producing whatever it sees fit, with each farmer doing more or less whatsoever he wishes with the income. The amount of cooperation is determined by the inhabitants of each moshav individually, on a democratic basis, but as a minimum there is cooperative buying and selling of raw materials and farm products, and cooperative running of certain services within the village itself.

The basic economic principles that developed around the establishment of the first moshav in 1921 continue today: mutual aid, cooperative buying and selling, farming on national land that cannot be bought or sold, and farming without the use of hired labor.

These principles emphasize that on the family farms of the moshav the necessary labor for their operation should come from the family unit itself. There is no hiring of labor, which, theoretically, is prohibited save in the case of illness. It is also assumed that no outside employment will be necessary to maintain the farmer and his family, and that he will be able to derive an adequate livelihood, comparable to that of other sectors of the national labor force.

Another tenet of moshav organization is the use of land owned by the Jewish National Fund, a public body originally established to purchase land in Palestine. This land can only be leased from the moshav, and the individual farmer cannot sell, pledge, or mortage it. It can only be rented, or exchanged, with another farmer in the same moshav, and then only with the permission of the Village Committee. This again stresses the egalitarian principle that one farmer should not be able to acquire more land than another. While individual differences are recognized, and individual initiative is encouraged, one farmer should not expand his economy at the expense of his fellows. This last idea is also reflected in the principles of mutual aid and cooperative buying and marketing of products of the farmers of the village. Cooperative purchasing and selling ensures that there will be sufficient capital for the municipality to carry out its public activities; that at the same time the individual farmer will receive goods more cheaply by buying in large quantities; and that the sales of farmers will contribute to the general good. The moshav provides various services for its members, such as a school, a synagogue, roads, a general store, and so forth, depending upon the wealth of the group and the demands of the individual members.

Mutual aid is an integral part of the moshav ideology: each farmer is responsible for his fellows and must aid them in time of need, as in illness. And the basic assumption is that adherence to these principles will guarantee all farmers an adequate, and more or less equal, income.

The municipality is governed by the members themselves through the General Assembly of all members, by the Village Committee, and by various other committees elected by the members of the community. If individual disputes cannot be settled informally, they may be taken to the Village Committee for settlement. If the Village Committee cannot or will not settle the matter, disputes can be taken to the General Assembly, and if the decision still proves to be unsatisfactory, it can be appealed to the Moshav Federation, which has final powers.

Moshavim were established for both ideological and economic reasons. The ideology emphasized cooperation in the struggle to create an egalitarian Jewish society. Economically, the moshav was important because, by cooperating on a collective basis in various stages of production, the community of farmers with limited capital could operate more efficiently. Since the moshavim were established at a time of food scarcity in Palestine, there were no restraints placed upon farmers to increase their output, within the limits of the moshav ideology. On the contrary, farmers could develop and increase output to the limits of their ability, so long as they did not compete with other members of their community.

Since the founding of the State of Israel, the moshav has taken on a somewhat different role and has been subject to different pressures as a consequence of the changes that have taken place within Israeli society in general and particularly within its agricultural organization. A surplus of agricultural products since the mid-1950's has resulted in the introduction of farm policies, with increased planning by the Ministry of Agriculture and the Settlement Department of the Jewish Agency. These changes have played an important part in placing stresses on many aspects of moshav organization. Restrictions have been imposed on agricultural production through the imposition of quotas, subsidies, and control of the flow of investment capital. These limitations are acutely felt by the farmers within moshavim, since they have been forced to change their farm crops to keep in line with governmental policies and changes in market prices.

Under these conditions, labor pioneering and other Zionist motivations are no longer sufficient justification for settling on the land. There has been an increased demand for efficiency in farming and for the introduction of new methods and techniques. Although agriculture is subsidized to a high degree by the government, there are severe strains on governmental resources in other areas, particularly in defense, which make the continued subsidizing of agriculture an important issue. Agriculture has now reached the point where it must pay for itself, or the system must be changed.

Moshav Sharon

Against this background, an economic dispute among the farmers of Sharon, a small moshav in central Israel, provides important evidence. Sharon was created as a moshav in 1948, immediately after Israel's War of Independence. Generally most post-Independence moshavim were made up of newly arrived immigrants from Arab countries, people who had no ideological interest in socialism or equality. However, this was not the situation in Sharon. Almost all of the men who helped to found this moshav, or who now live in the community, spent some time in a kibbutz or other moshav before coming to Sharon. Approximately 15 per cent had been born in Israel, and all had spent some years in Israel before arriving in the village. Thus, most had been committed at one time or another to the ideals of collectivism or cooperation.

The moshav itself is divided into 68 family farms of approximately 30 *dunams* each (approximately 7½ acres). Initially each farmer was given equal amounts of livestock, tools, a modest house and furnishings, plus financial and agricultural assistance by the Settlement Department of the Jewish Agency. The farmers were encouraged to develop mixed farms, farms with a diversity of farm branches, in order to spread the labor requirements for the farm more evenly throughout the year. In this way the farmer would not be dependent upon only one farm branch for his income in case of changes in market conditions. Thus, at one time there were 60 men in Sharon with small dairy herds; almost everyone had chickens for egg production and newly planted orange trees, and most grew vegetables as well.

Over time, because of each farmer's social and economic capital and as a result of the developments within Israeli agriculture, farmers began emphasizing one farm branch and minimizing others. Most men began to invest heavily in citrus because of government support and the high prices received, and reduced or eliminated vegetable production because of the low market prices for these commodities. By the time of this investigation, 1966–1968, although most farmers had at least two farm branches on their farms, the relative importance of these branches was generally not equal. While there were 33 dairy farmers in Sharon at this time, the over-all value to each farmer varied considerably. For example, the seven large-scale dairy producers had, on average, 19.1 cattle units,[5] requiring 385 workdays, the sixteen middle-sized producers averaged 12.1 cattle units and 275 workdays, while the ten small-scale producers averaged only 9.0 cattle units and 242 workdays per year. Thus the over-all investment by the large-scale producers was twice that of the small-scale pro-

---

[5] Cattle units are calculated in the following manner: a cow with a yield of less than 4,500 liters/year = 0.9 cattle units; a cow with a yield of 4,501–5,500 liters/year = 1.0 cattle units; a cow with a yield of more than 5,500 liters/year = 1.1 cattle units; female calves and heifers, each = 0.45 cattle units; and bull calves, each = 0.50 cattle units (see *Institute of Farm Income Research*, 1967).

ducers, and about 50 per cent greater than the middle-sized dairy producers.

The Dispute

By the mid-1960's, because of the general overproduction of milk throughout Israel, the Ministry of Agriculture developed milk quotas for each agricultural settlement, based upon its previous production. For each moshav this village quota had to be divided among the producers, by the farmers themselves. The members of the Village Committee of Sharon had been delaying forcing a decision upon the dairymen over the division of the milk quota. It was common practice in the moshav to refrain from manifesting disputes or potential disputes as long as possible, so that formal confrontations could be avoided. In this way open hostility would be suppressed and the community would not be split apart, even if temporarily. However, pressure was building up to force the dairy farmers in Sharon to curtail their milk output. The village's milk quota of 1,270,000 liters, which was to remain constant until 1971, had been reached. The village had reached its quota by the spring of 1967, and in the ensuing months was actually overproducing. The government was threatening to withhold its subsidy both on the milk produced and on the grain for the cows' dry fodder. A General Assembly meeting was called to discuss the problem and decide on a formula for the distribution of the quota among the farmers.

The Village Committee called the meeting. Committeemen decided to put forth their own solution to the problem of apportionment of the milk quota. At this time, only two members of the seven-man Village Committee were dairymen, and generally they did not have a strong influence on decisions taken in Committee meetings. The Committee felt that it was being most reasonable and objective in its proposal for the distribution of the milk quota. The Village Committee's proposal was as follows: 1,000,000 liters would be divided among those who had dairy herds at present, while the remainder of the quota would be kept in a pool for those who might begin new dairy herds, such as farmers' sons returning from Army service who might want to begin milk production. The proposal would also put a limit of 60,000 liters on the amount that could be produced by any one farmer and still receive the government subsidy. In case the pooled milk reserve was not used up, the other farmers could divide it among themselves, with the price received dependent on the total amount produced above 1,000,000 liters. This would establish a two-price structure: a guaranteed price for each farmer up to 60,000 liters and a pooled price thereafter. That is, above the 60,000 liters a farmer could receive no subsidy on his milk. Only three dairymen had produced more than 60,000 liters in the previous year, and only three others had come close to this figure. The average for the 33 dairymen was 38,510 liters.

The meeting was scheduled to begin at 8:30 in the evening, during the middle of the week. Like every other meeting of the General Assembly of the village, this one began 45 minutes late, when there finally were 20 members present. Only 12 of the 33 dairymen in Sharon attended.

The Village Treasurer, an outsider employed by the community, was the chairman of the meeting. He explained to the Assembly the problem of overproduction and the need for apportionment of the milk quota, and he then went into some detail about government policy on the matter. The Treasurer then presented, without comment, the proposal of the Village Committee on the distribution of the milk quota and called for discussion.

The Village Committee's proposal was immediately attacked by Aaron, a small-scale dairy producer and a politically powerful member of Sharon, a man often looked upon as one of the spokesmen for the dairymen. Aaron proposed that the entire quota be divided among everyone, that everyone should share equally, and that nothing be held back in reserve. His idea was that every dairyman should get a quota of 35,000 liters of milk each year.

Gideon, Aaron's neighbor, suggested a modification both of the Village Committee's proposal and of Aaron's. He wanted a ceiling to be set on the pooled price at 50,000 liters, while guaranteeing each dairyman 35,000 liters. The amount anyone produced between 35,000 and 50,000 would receive the pooled price. Anything above 50,000 liters would receive the marginal price, if all of the pool of milk was used up. This would have made it possible for a large-scale dairy producer to receive three different prices for his milk: the guaranteed price, which was the full government subsidy; the pooled price, which might be less than the government subsidy if the village and the individual farmer went beyond 35,000 liters; and the marginal price, if the farmer went beyond 50,000 liters, while the village as a whole went beyond its milk quota. The marginal price of milk was so low that the farmer would be losing money for each liter he produced.

At this point, I must clarify some points about the framework in which public discussions take place in Sharon. Regardless of the growing dissatisfaction of these farmers with many of the basic economic premises of the moshav, in public discussions the welfare of the community over the individual was an important consideration. In every discussion of public concern in Sharon, the proposal or argument put forward must demonstrate that the individual farmer is not out only

for himself, or for his interest group, but is also concerned
with the interests of all of his fellows. If he does not show
such concern, his proposals may never succeed. Some men in
Sharon have a reputation for being out for their own self-
interest, while others are seen as being fair and objective to all
in the moshav. During the discussion of the milk quotas, all
put forward proposals couched in terms of what to them was
the fairest and most objective way of distributing the milk
quota for the general welfare.

In fact, the Village Committee's proposal was more generous than either Aaron's or Gideon's, because the Committee
felt that the large-scale producers, who were responsible for
the size of the quota in the first place, should not be greatly
penalized. When Aaron put forward his proposal, he said that
no one in the village should profit at the expense of others and
everyone should have a fair share. Gideon agreed with Aaron,
but he thought that the large-scale dairymen would be too
severely punished with a quota as low as Aaron had suggested.
Aaron then amended his proposal and agreed with Gideon
that perhaps Gideon's proposition was more equitable.

Isaac was the only large-scale milk producer who spoke
during the discussion. He began by stating his opposition to
the idea of a ceiling on milk production. He wanted to prevent anyone else from beginning a new dairy herd, and suggested that the quota should be divided on a different basis.
Why, he argued, should there be a pool of the milk quota
kept in reserve if this had not been done either with the distribution of land in the small orange grove quota or with the
distribution of the egg quota. He went on to attack the assumption that the quota should be spread equally among all
of the dairymen, since, he argued, the quota had been granted
to the moshav because of the amount of milk produced by

farmers like himself and other big producers. Now that the quota had been given, should he be punished and made to reduce his output while someone else would benefit at his expense?

When he had finished speaking Isaac was reproached by some of the men at the meeting for misrepresenting the distribution of the milk and egg quotas to the village. (Isaac has a reputation in the village for penury and for individualistic behavior in a most negative sense.) He was not directly accused by Aaron of putting his own interests above that of others, but for his seeming unwillingness to give others, who were in economic difficulties, the opportunity of beginning a dairy herd if they wished. They argued that he had not even suggested a reasonable course of action.

After this dispute, Roni, the only member of the Village Committee present and a nondairyman, spoke briefly to defend the Committee's proposal which he said was the fairest. The discussion ended shortly afterwards with only one other person giving his opinion on a peripheral issue. After this, a vote was called. It was to be either for the proposal of the Village Committee or for the proposal of Aaron and Gideon, the decision to last for one year after which time it would be reviewed.

The Assembly voted 7-5 in favor of the Aaron-Gideon proposal, with all other members present at the meeting abstaining. In view of the importance of the decision to the other members of the moshav it may seem strange that there were not more people present, especially dairymen, and that one faction did not try to garner a larger vote for its proposal. No formal attempt had been made to organize voters in advance nor to persuade supporters to attend the meeting. Most farmers appeared indifferent over the outcome of this critical decision.

An Analysis of the Farmers' Behavior—Differences of Interest

Any explanation for this kind of behavior must lie in the nature of political action and in the manner and style of the making of political decisions within the Sharon moshav. The dairymen had known for a long time before this meeting that they would have to reach a decision on the allocation of the milk quota. (I have been talking only about the dairymen because, although theoretically everyone can vote on all matters at these meetings, in fact Roni, the representative of the Village Committee, was the only nondairyman at the meeting to cast a vote.) Thus the dairymen had had time to talk and debate the best solution to their problem. During these pre-meeting discussions they had agreed informally on a general policy, although, as was apparent at the meeting, they had not drawn up any definite prearranged proposal. Thus, though the vote was small in terms of numbers, four of the five most powerful and influential dairymen were present at the meetings, and three of them voted together for the winning proposal. Their vote represented the decision that had already been reached and agreed upon informally and in general terms by a majority of the dairymen. The dispute had actually been settled by the dairymen themselves before the meeting took place.

The arguments for the proposals were all couched in terms of fairness to the community at large as opposed to individual gain at the expense of the collectivity, but an analysis of the vote, despite its smallness, reveals some interesting details. The vote was clearly determined by economic self-interest, ideological declarations notwithstanding. Differences between the interests of the large producers and the small ones were basic. Those small producers who voted with the major producers were men who intended to expand their cattle holdings. Voting on the other side were the smaller producers and those who had no plans for expansion. Factors affecting plans for expanding production were the age of the farmer and the stage of the family cycle at which he found himself, since hiring labor was forbidden by moshav principles, and the family was the principal source of workers. There is a significant difference between the mean ages of the five men who voted for the Village Committee's proposal (mean age, 36.4) and the seven men who voted for Aaron's and Gideon's proposal (mean age, 52.6). In other words, those who voted for the Village Committee's proposal (larger guaranteed quota) were much younger than those who voted for Aaron's and Gideon's proposal. The largest milk producer in Sharon, Haim, sat through the meeting by himself, but he neither took part in the discussion nor voted. The only two large-scale dairy producers present who voted both did so for the Committee's proposals—which would have given them a greater guaranteed quota. The other three men to vote for the Committee's proposal were both in what is called the Middle Phase of family development,[6] and possessed small-scale dairy farms that were producing little at the time, but these were in the process of being expanded.

[6] The phases of family development emphasize the availability of labor within the family in relation to economic demands. For example: Early Phase = all children are under 15, or if there are no children, the farmer's wife is still young enough (under age 45) to have children; Middle Phase = some of the children are of working age (15–18), live at home, and work on or off the farm; Late Phase = all of the children have left home, or the wife is past child-bearing age and has no children (for further elaboration see Nalson, 1968).

The seven men who voted for the Aaron-Gideon proposal were all above the age of 45, and four were over 50 years old. Five were in the Middle Phase of family development and two were in the Late Phase. None of these men had large-sized dairy farms: only two had produced more than 35,000 liters of milk during the previous year, the highest being 41,000 liters. From interviews with these men I know that *none was interested in any great expansion of his milk output,* as this would involve more work. All of these men had sons who were in the Army or who were about to enter the Army for their three years of military service, and none was sure what the future held for them in terms of their sons' desire to return to farming. They were interested in consolidating their position and in guaranteeing a minimum income for themselves. This factor can be observed in the significantly greater investment in citrus by the seven who voted for the Aaron-Gideon proposal against the five for Committee's proposal: 17.2 *dunams* against 14.2 *dunams,* respectively. This vote reflects a split within the association of dairy farmers: between the younger and older dairymen; between those with large herds and high aspirations against those with smaller herds who wanted to insure a guaranteed, basic income from milk production. Since these older men with small and middle-sized dairy farms dominate both numerically and politically in Sharon, they carried the vote, even if by only 2 votes, and even though only one-sixth of the eligible voters voted.

Are the proposals very different? Basically they are not unlike one another. The Committee's proposal for limiting output to 60,000 liters would affect only the three farmers who had produced above 60,000 liters the previous year. The Aaron-Gideon proposal on the other hand, not only limits the individual quota to 50,000 liters a year but also guarantees the price up to 35,000 liters. The difference concerns conditions, not at present, but in the future. With the Committee's proposal, if all of the present 33 dairymen produced close to the recommended quota of 60,000 liters, there would be a considerable surplus of milk for the village. This would mean that the village would have to pool the price it received for milk, combining the guaranteed price from the government for the quota of milk with the marginal price for surplus milk, thus considerably reducing the price of milk to all of the dairymen in Sharon. The Aaron-Gideon proposal, on the other hand, guaranteed the basic minimum on 35,000 liters. This was more than the amount produced by most of those who voted for this proposal. There were in the whole community only seven dairymen who produced more than 50,000 liters in the 1966–1967 season. The only two who were present voted for the Committee's proposal.

The actual economic self-interest evident in this situation had to be rationalized within the ideology, placing the interests of the collectivity above those of the individual. This problem of economic equality and inequality in economic development is a difficult dilemma to solve in a moshav. Usually it can be masked. But it surfaces in this situation in a troublesome and public form because of the impingement of the milk quota on farmers who possess farms of different sizes and have diverse aspirations.

When Isaac stated in the meeting that the quota would not have been as high as it was if it were not for large producers like himself, he was advancing this point: Is it fair then that the large producers should be made to lose at the expense of those who were less able than themselves?

After the meeting was over, Haim, the biggest dairyman in Sharon, got up and left by himself, without speaking to anyone. Throughout the meeting he had quietly sat alone. Haim had produced over 80,000 liters of milk during the previous year, and he had continued with this output during the time when the quota was imposed. No matter which proposal was to be accepted he was going to have to curtail his output or risk heavy financial losses on the milk he produced above his individual quota, so long as the village as a whole produced above its quota. Haim is not only the biggest dairyman in Sharon, he is also among the most efficient. Rather than reduce the size of his output, he wanted to increase it, modernize his equipment, and enlarge his cowshed.

When I spoke to him later, Haim emphasized that if the village decided that he could not produce more than 35,000 or 50,000 liters of milk a year, then he would ask the Village Committee to give him the part of the milk quota he felt was owed to him, since his large output was partially responsible for the size of the present quota. Using the same argument as Isaac, Haim pointed out that if it were not for him and other large producers the village would not have such a large quota. He added that three men were considering giving up their cows, since, if he and others did not keep up their production, even increase it, the village as a whole would produce less, and the milk quota would actually be reduced. Haim had shifted his argument to bring it more into the general ideological framework that is presented in public discussions in Sharon, indicating that by increasing production, he would be acting for the general welfare.

Conclusion

The controversy over the division of the milk quota brought into open dispute at least two bodies of conflicting interests within the association of dairy farmers: the first faction con-

tains the younger, more aggressive, and still ambitious dairymen, who are seeking some way of increasing their produc-
tivity; and the second faction represents the older, small, or
middle-sized dairy producers who are seeking only to maintain their production and assure their income. This diversity
of economic interests is recognized by all of the farmers in
Sharon. They speak of the dairymen as an interest group or
association, but they also recognize that there are factions
within this association. This understanding allowed the Village Committee, made up primarily of nondairymen, to present
its proposal as the most equitable and objective to both the
large and small producers. Equally significant was the recognition by the community of the dairymen's right to settle this
problem among themselves, just as the vegetable growers and
orange growers settle theirs. Certainly there is nothing in
moshav ideology that sanctions this policy, or even encourages it. The lack of attendance at the meeting and the absten-
tion from voting by those nondairymen who were present indicates the acknowledgment of this development.

The recognition of specific interest groups and the legitimacy of allowing them to settle certain disputes among themselves is the result of significant economic changes within
Sharon. On the other hand, the heterogeneity of individual
economic interests is such that, while men are competing on
one issue, they are cooperating in another. While the kind of
economic issue described here could be seen as pulling a segment of the village apart, it has also prevented the formation
of dominant political or economic associations within the village. It is the factionalist and outside interests among the
dairymen that divide them and at the same time establish
crosscutting ties throughout the moshav. The dairymen are
forced to compete among themselves in one instance, while at

another time they become aware of their more overriding, common interests when they have to compete against other economic groups for their own common goals. These differences in individual interests thus prevent many disputes from leading to open, permanent cleavages within the community.

This particular dispute opened up the problem of the individual versus the collective in a cooperative society with a strong egalitarian basis, and raised the question of how much the individual must subordinate his initiative for the benefit of fellow farmers in his village. Being in a minority, the large milk producers must not let it appear that they are putting their own self-interest above that of their fellows. I have tried to indicate that despite the rhetoric of egalitarianism used by those who voted for the Aaron-Gideon proposal, they too acted in terms of their own self-interest, which happened to be that of the majority of the dairymen of the village.

The premise that individual actions are governed by self-interest suggests that, within certain ideological or normatively defined limits, individuals try to maximize their own advantage within the social situation as they see it. This kind of explanation does not mean that norms or ideology have little or no meaning, that they are used only for manipulation. What it does imply is that the norms themselves do not combine to form a cohesive system. Rather, as Turner (1957) has pointed out, there are conflicts and ambiguities and even contradictions within all systems. This idea applies even to those that are carefully planned. It is precisely because of these normative conflicts that individuals are able to manipulate their social situations. It was exactly because of these conflicts in the tenets of the moshav that different men, with different interests, could attempt to influence their fellows with ideological arguments regarding the merits of their position.

While the majority of dairy farmers could correctly maintain that their proposal for the distribution of the milk quota was more equitable for the majority and would give every diary farmer the opportunity to earn a profitable income, the large-scale dairymen could also maintain that the quota that was given to the village was based on their output and that they were being punished for being more efficient than the others. Each of these positions is not of equal ideological merit. The small-scale farmers did not win out simply because they were in the majority. The majority proposal was accepted because, within the then current economic conditions, this was the most acceptable solution within the general premises of moshav ideology and organization. These men realize that, while at one time cooperation was an end in itself in the ideology of the moshav, with the changed economic situation in which they now find themselves, cooperation has become a technique for efficiency, not an end in itself. At a later time, with changed economic circumstances, this proposal might not be carried, and the ideology and organizational principles might have to be manipulated in a different manner.

REFERENCES

Baldwin, Elaine. 1972. Differentiation and Cooperation in an Israeli Veteran Moshav. Manchester: Manchester University Press.

Eisenstadt, S. N. 1954. The Absorption of Immigrants. London: Routledge & Kegan Paul.

——. 1956. Sociological Aspects of the Economic Adaptation of Oriental Immigrants in Israel. Economic Development and Cultural Change 4.

——. 1967. Israeli Society. London: Weidenfeld and Nicolson.

Gluckman, Max. 1961. Ethnographic Data in British Social Anthropology. Sociological Review 9:5–17.

Institute of Farm Income Research. 1967. The Profitability of Various Farm Branches in Israel in the Agricultural Year 1964/1965. Tel Aviv: Government publishers.

Leon, Dan. 1969. The Kibbutz. London: Pergamon Press.

Nalson, J. S. 1968. Mobility of Farm Families. Manchester: Manchester University Press.

Shokeid, M. 1971. The Dual Heritage. Manchester: Manchester University Press.

Spiro, M. 1956. Kibbutz: Venture in Utopia. Cambridge: Harvard University Press.

Talmon-Garber, Y. 1962. The Family in Collective Settlements. In Transactions of the Fifth World Congress of Sociology, Vol. 4.

——. 1965. The Family in a Revolutionary Movement. In M. Nimkoff, ed. Comparative Family Systems. New York: Houghton Mifflin.

Talmon-Garber, Y. and E. Cohen. 1964. Collective Settlements in the Negev. In J. Ben-David, ed. Agricultural Planning and Village Community in Israel. Paris: UNESCO.

Turner, Victor. 1957. Schism and Continuity in an African Society. Manchester: Manchester University Press.

Van Velsen, J. 1967. The Extended-Case Method and Situational Analysis. In A. L. Epstein, ed. The Craft of Social Anthropology. London: Tavistock.

Weingarten, M. 1955. Life in a Kibbutz. New York: Reconstructionist Press.

Weingrod, Alex. 1966. Reluctant Pioneers: Village Development in Israel. Ithaca: Cornell University Press.

Weintraub, Dov. 1964. A Study of New Farmers in Israel. Sociologia Ruralis 4:1.

Weintraub, D., and M. Lissak. 1961. The Absorption of North African Immigrants in Agricultural Settlements in Israel. Jewish Journal of Sociology 3:29–54.

——. 1964. Physical and Material Conditions in New Moshavin. In Joseph Ben-David, ed. Agricultural Planning and Village Community in Israel. Paris: UNESCO.

CHAPTER 5

Stigma, Ostracism, and Expulsion in an Israeli Kibbutz[1]

TERENCE M. S. EVENS

The kibbutzim are Israeli collective settlements whose members view their society as an attempt to realize a particular ideology, the two main components of which (for the great majority of these communities) are socialism and Zionism. Such communities show a variety of organizational principles, but collectivism is pre-eminent.

From November, 1965, to May, 1967, I worked in one such community, called here Kibbutz Timem. Although Zionist, Timem identifies with the Left in Israel; it also rejects ortho-

[1] I wish to thank the Bernstein Israeli Research Trust of the Department of Social Anthropology at Manchester University for supporting the field research on which this paper is based. The case dealt with here is ethically sensitive. For this reason I have altered its contents, so that, like the names employed, it is fictitious. The analysis, however, is based on the original data. I should also point out that, the actual case, described as a course of events, is far from typical of the kibbutz's everyday social life. In fact, as Durkheim taught, it is because it is "pathological" that it can illuminate fundamental aspects of the kibbutz that would otherwise be difficult of access. Finally, at the risk of being presumptuous, I should like to warn the reader against making too facile an ethical judgment. In view of the kibbutz presenting itself as an alternative society, the case invites such a judgment. But perhaps the case itself is sufficient warning.

dox Judaism. During the time I was there, it numbered about 600 persons, 300 of whom were members or *chaverim;* most of the others were members' children. The community was settled in its present location in Israel's fertile Jezreel Valley in 1929. Its original founders were Polish immigrants, and the great majority of those immigrants who joined subsequently were also Eastern European (though not all Polish). Timem's economy is based on highly mechanized mixed farming and a plastics industry.

Before describing and analyzing the case, I should define some terms and introduce some theoretical concepts. By "stigma" I mean, following Goffman (1968:11f.), an attribute constituting a special discrepancy between the socially legitimized expectations of person and the actuality of person. By "ostracism" I refer to any form of social exclusion. By "expulsion" I mean the extreme form of ostracism. "Social embarrassment," "social identity," and "personal identity" belong also to Goffman's terminology, and except for "embarrassment," I follow his usage.

Failure to measure up to ideals and expectations and the desire to surmount such failure in the future is communicated as "embarrassment." Goffman restricts "embarrassment" to the individual, but here the concept is stretched to cover also the plural person (Goffman, 1956). The kibbutz can be embarrassed. It can communicate its corporate embarrassment by vacillating over what to do in the case of some departure from the ideal, or simply by admitting failure to realize an ideal. In general, however, by regulating and controlling information on deviation or failure, the kibbutz shows potential embarrassment.[2]

---

[2] Somewhere in his massive and splendid study (1968), Schurmann

By "social identity" I mean those social roles and attributes held appropriate to an individual. Clearly, the concept is like that of social status (see Goffman, 1968:12, 73f., for what he sees as the difference), and I use it here because it seems the best term analogous to "personal identity." By "personal identity" I refer to those attributes of an individual that render him unique and differentiate him from others. These attributes include what Goffman (1968:74) calls "identity pegs"—for example, appearance or walk, and items of biography; for any individual the combination of these is unique.

Two points may now be made. One: because the kibbutz ideology is focused on a synthesis of the individual and the collective, a focus which the kibbutz social organization reflects sharply, the individual's personal identity is profoundly conflated with his social identity. As a result, his failure to conform to normative expectations is likely to involve collective as well as personal embarrassment. Two: given the first point, and because the endeavor to unite the individual and the collective makes very great demands on him, the kibbutz may be expected to exhibit a high incidence of potential collective embarrassment. Durkheim says (1938:68–69):

Imagine a society of saints, a perfect cloister of exemplary individuals. Crimes, properly so-called, will there be unknown; but faults which appear venial to the layman will create there the same scandal that the ordinary offense does in ordinary consciousnesses. If, then, this society has the power to judge and punish, it will define these acts as criminal and will treat them as such. For the same reason, the perfect and upright man judges his smallest failings with a severity that the majority reserve for acts more truly in the nature of an offense.

---

remarks on Communist China's failure to disclose to the outside world the progress of social experiments until after their success is assured.

The Case and Its Formal Proceedings

In June 1966, Timem's Secretary informed me that Kete-myeh, one of Timem's members had decided to marry a girl who lived in a nearby town. Ketemyeh was a thirty-year old "son-of-the-kibbutz" who worked in the community's "residential gardening." His fiancée was described as an immigrant from Iraq; it was also mentioned that she was a divorcee. The Secretary went on to say that Timem's Secretariat—the administrative organ of which he was head and whose authority was second only to the community's General Assembly—had concluded that this girl was not "kibbutz material" and could have no place in Timem. The Secretariat had therefore proposed that if Ketemyeh should proceed with his marriage, he and his bride would not be allowed to reside in Timem. The Secretariat had also moved, however, that should the community decide to exclude the couple residentially, then it should also undertake to insure the couple's support, and Ketemyeh should be allowed to continue in his job at Timem. In informing me, the Secretary's purpose was to ask me not to attend the next meeting of Timem's General Assembly in which the issue of Ketemyeh's marriage was to be raised, for the meeting, he said, was going to be a miserable affair.[3]

The issue was brought to the next General Assembly (which meets weekly on Saturday nights).[4] The Secretariat

[3] In anticipating that the meeting would be a 'miserable one,' the Secretary meant that unpleasant remarks about particular individuals were likely to be made. He was expressing a reserve generally felt in the community about the public airing of personal issues (*seifim ishiim*), indicating that there was some dissatisfaction over the lack of insulation between a man's personal and social identities.

[4] Clearly, as I was more or less prohibited from attending this and a second General Assembly meeting on the issue, I had to rely on

presented the issue in terms of two options—either to permit the couple to reside in Timem for a probationary period of a few months, or to insist from the outset that the couple take up residence outside Timem, with the provision that Timem would support them and Ketemyeh would be permitted to continue in his job. The Secretariat went on record as favoring the "hard decision": immediate external residence. The argument of the Secretariat was that the girl was not kibbutz material. In this connection, it was stressed that she was illiterate. At some point Ketemyeh's father accused the Secretary of bias in his assessment of the girl. Indeed, I was told that he accused the Secretariat of racism, that is, of rejecting the girl because she was Iraqi. Probably as a result of this charge, an ad hoc committee was appointed to investigate further.

Three weeks later the issue was raised again when the ad hoc committee stated its decision: that it approved of the girl, but that, assessing the mood of the community, it had concluded that the Secretariat's proposal of immediate external residence was best. Ketemyeh's supporters argued principally that it was by precedent the right of every member to bring a spouse to Timem from the outside for probationary membership. Throughout the meeting—indeed for the duration of the case—Ketemyeh's opponents took great pains to persuade Ketemyeh's father especially of the reasonableness of their option. In voting, a majority favored the Secretariat's and the ad hoc committee's position: that the couple should take up external residence upon their marriage, that Timem would support the couple, and that Ketemyeh would continue at Timem as a gardener. As it turned out, Ketemyeh eventually

informants. These were highly reliable, however, though of course I should have preferred more detailed information.

declined the offer of his job, and with his bride moved else-where to live near relatives in another part of Israel.

It should be said that the proposition that the girl was not kibbutz material is by no means as vague as the formal pro-ceedings might suggest. During the public airing of the issue, a number of derogatory things about the girl were rumored in Timem. It was said that her uncle had raped his daughter, that her family was dishonest, that she herself was an "idiot," and that she was very ugly. Also, pejorative comments were overheard concerning the girl's being an "oriental" (hence Ketemyeh's father's accusation of racism). And, the girl's being a divorcee was apparently regarded as indicative of her supposed inferiority. Obviously, such opinions discredited her social and personal identities. And although these opinions were not formally aired (How could they have been without questioning the legitimacy of the issue?), they were nonethe-less tacit ingredients of Ketemyeh's opponents' position that she was not kibbutz material, and that the mood of the com-munity favored immediate external residence for the couple.

Some five months after the General Assembly's decision had been taken, I was told that a legal contract between the kibbutz and the couple was being drawn up to insure the couple of support for life. I was also told that it stipulated, in the event of the death of either Ketemyeh or his wife, that the surviving mate had the right to take up residence in the kibbutz with the children of the union, should there be any. I should add, however, that my informant was not directly involved with the processing of the contract, and it is possible that my information is not accurate or complete.

The description of the case raises two questions which are the analytical focus of this essay: First, why did Ketemyeh's

proposed marriage become an issue? Second, for what reason
was the couple residentially excluded?

Clearly, the reason given by the community for the decision, that is, that the girl was not kibbutz material, directly
concerns these questions. But, although what were considered
the girl's undesirable social and personal characteristics apparently explain the case in full, in fact the case has other
dimensions. The inadequacy of the community's explanation
for the turn of events is apparent, for virtually nothing is said
about the community's unusual decision to support the couple
and legally bind itself in this regard. A satisfactory explanation must elucidate these features too. But, as I will later
show, the issue of the girl does in an important way enter into
the explanation.

The formal proceedings contain another aspect of explanation, though it is difficult to assess its importance. The arguments employed by (available to?) the two sides to legitimate
their respective positions afforded Ketemyeh's opponents the
advantage. Citing the mood of the community, they appealed
to a principle ideologically superior to that represented by
the right of an individual member to bring in a spouse. The
latter refers to the rights of the individual as a distributive
unit, whereas the former refers to his rights as an aggregative
unit: it goes to the core of the community's principles, the
right of the whole to decide as it sees fit, even if this means
putting aside other regular but less basic rights.

It is well to keep two points in mind for the analysis to follow. First, the formal airing of the case focused on the girl,
not on Ketemyeh. Explicitly, the matter was viewed as a rejection of the girl's application for membership, not as an expulsion of Ketemyeh—Ketemyeh's residential departure was
defined as a consequence of his intention to marry a girl

found undesirable by the community. Second, the initiative to exclude Ketemyeh and the girl was taken formally by the Secretariat, a body whose organizational importance as representative of the whole is second only to that of the General Assembly. Moreover, the ad hoc committee, appointed to represent the social whole on the issue, in supporting the Secretariat's decision spoke also in the name of the community. This committee said its duty was to make its decision comport with the mood of the community. In other words, the proposal to exclude the couple was associated with the opinion of the whole and was not to be interpreted as personal preference. Indeed, Ketemyeh's father's charge that the Secretary was biased may be viewed as an attempt to discredit the Secretariat's claim to have decided on behalf of the whole.

Social Structure

Social relationships in Timem proceed in accordance with a number of structural, categorical, and interpersonal principles. These include occupation, administration, consanguineous and affinal kinship, age, sex, generational seniority of membership, neighborhood, leisure-time interests, and interpersonal exchange (visiting and exchanging of books, cigarettes, gossip, cash, and other favors). Thus the community is structurally characterized by a wide variety of labor branches and administrative committees; by small, named groups of age peers; and by families, some comprising three generations; by social categories based respectively on sex, generation, age, seniority, and neighborhood (a conspicuous sexual division of labor exists; there is talk about "intergenerational conflict"; age and seniority are explicitly employed in the allocating of goods, housing, etc.; and there are five residential neighborhoods distinguishable by reference to locale and type of housing); and by small networks of links based on common leisure-time concerns and interpersonal exchange. In addition, there are a large number of ties that extend outside the community. These may be based on kinship, work, Federation politics, military service, artistic endeavors, and other principles, and, depending on the nature, these ties may be manipulated by members for internal purposes. Finally, it should be noted that these relational circumstances are further complicated by links whose history reaches beyond their current principles (for example, friends whose relationship was based originally on the sharing of a common neighborhood but who now reside in different neighborhoods).

The high degree to which Timem is internally differentiated bears comparison to any modern society, and is correlative with Timem's own modernity (industrialization, mechanization, occupational specialization, and so on). However, unlike the case in most modern situations, where the individual's several functionally separate and distinct social identities are segmental and relatively well-insulated from one another, under Timem's structural circumstances, owing to the radical collectivization and common administration of most relational spheres, the individual's various social identities are poorly insulated from one another. Put differently, because the role of kibbutz-member is meant to be organizationally synthetic and to represent the integration of all the relational spheres in a meaningful social world, the individual has great difficulty keeping his various social identities segregated.

Consider the rule of voting in Timem's General Assembly by show of hands. By virtue of this tradition, whereby the individual has no choice but to communicate his explicit political preference to all, relationships which are logically irrelevant to the political issue at question become factually relevant to his politics. (For example, take the member who, on grounds of merit, wants to vote against a particular candidate for some internal administrative office, but who chooses to do otherwise because his preference would be revealed to the candidate's wife, with whom he must daily work side by side.) Hence, a structural situation of apparent simplicity becomes simultaneously one of multiplicity. This circumstance bears comparison with the traditional, rather than modern society. The manner in which Timem's organization runs a course between two logically polar modes of solidarity, between tradition and modernity and between status and contract, respectively, is no accident; rather, it mirrors the kibbutz ideology's aim to unite the individual and the collective.

One result of this mode of social organization is the prevention of the emergence of any permanently solidary political groupings within the community. What one finds in Timem is that, generally speaking, each political issue, by activating a unique nexus of relational principles, creates factions specific to the issue itself.

Clearly, the individual member of Timem is likely to be sustained by a structural/categorical/interpersonal network of large scope, diversity, and interactional density, and to have a number of avenues for mobilizing support. However, owing to the high degree to which this collectivist organization makes relations accessible to all its members, the individual's network is transected complexly by the networks of others. As a result, diffusion of power in Timem—a prime aim of kibbutz ideology—is extensive.

Of course, this diffusion is not, nor could it be, complete. A situationally specific power differential always emerges. The greater the number of relationships in which a member participates and the more securely and advantageously he is established in each, the more generally powerful he is. For example, the member without a family in the community—and there are several such in Timem—is likely to be at a disadvantage, for he lacks the possibility of employing the old, extensive ties that such a family would have. The powerful member, by contrast, is able to gain support for himself and, what is more important, neutralize what would otherwise be support of his opponents. Indeed, voting in Timem's General Assembly is typically characterized by a large number of abstentions.

In addition, there are differences between members because some kinds of relationships are more powerful than others. For a variety of reasons, family relationships and occupational or administrative position are particularly important. Both, though especially family, strongly condition access to position elsewhere.

With these broad observations, it is possible to discuss Ketemyeh's social-structural circumstances. He was born a son-of-the-kibbutz in 1933. He was thus at the time of this study a senior member of Timem's second generation. He was raised in the kibbutz's educational system, along with the seven others of his age-peer group. Ketemyeh's group took formal membership in the community in 1953, when all were about twenty years old. In view of this, it is not unreasonable to suppose that, on the issue of his marriage, Ketemyeh should have been able to draw on a few strong dyadic relationships with members of this group. But as far as I could tell, he was not. Nor was he able to rely on much support from the categorical sympathies of age, generation, and seniority, which is also curious, considering that he was a first-born son-of-the-kibbutz.

As for interpersonal ties, it is noteworthy that Ketemyeh's interaction with his neighbors was, to my knowledge (I resided in the same neighborhood), unusually limited; nor did I ever observe him at private parties. It is likely that he had ties that I failed to observe, but I suspect he spent most of his leisure time with his parents. He did referee an informal ball game once a week. But this could hardly have afforded him support on the sensitive issue of his marriage.

There remain the factors of occupation/administration and family. According to my data (gleaned from the community's official records), Ketemyeh had never during his entire career in Timem held an administrative office, nor do I know that he ever sat on one of the community's many committees. These circumstances are anomalous for, owing to the large number of committees and offices in Timem, at any time the administration includes 50 per cent of the community's membership. What is more, these offices and committees rotate every one or two years.

Ketemyeh's occupation was residential gardening. Each fiscal year in Timem, labor branches are ranked according to their profits. As a result, the branches acquire differential importance and leverage in the community. Furthermore, because of the ideological stress on productive labor, and on the part's contribution to the whole, revenue-producing branches in contrast to service branches are accorded high value (cf. Kanovsky, 1966:45f.).

Clearly, residential gardening could not rate highly. Even among Timem's various services, it has small prestige. A service such as child-rearing which is entrusted with cultivating the minds meant to perpetuate the community, wields for this

reason considerable power. But gardening has no such cre-
dentials. The fact that it employs a crew of three, each usually working on his own, one a hired Arab laborer, testifies to
its political weakness.

Ketemyeh's participation in gardening was, then, indicative
of his own powerlessness. He had been in gardening from
1954—which suggests his political disadvantage was long-
standing. I often observed him at his job, and he usually
worked alone or with the hired laborer. In a community
where the ideology extols the camaraderie of working together in productive pursuits, the person who works in isolation at an inferior task presents a strikingly negative image.
Ketemyeh's job both conditioned and symbolized his social
enfeeblement.

Nor did Ketemyeh as yet have any family of procreation
which could have helped gain him support. The others in his
age-peer group were already married, and some had teen-age
children. Indeed, Ketemyeh's decision to start a family was a
bid to realize social and political normalcy, and it is what
made his case an issue.

Ketemyeh did, however, have his father in the community.
And it was on him that he relied in the dispute. Considering
that he was weak in other respects, and that the case concerned the future of his family in Timem, it is no wonder that
his defense fell on his father.

Ketemyeh's mother had died in 1957. He had an older
brother and a younger sister, but the former had renounced
membership and left in 1962, and at the time the case was
decided the latter was in the Army, and not yet a formal
member. Although neither of Ketemyeh's parents had been
among the very first settlers of Kibbutz Timem, both had

come soon after its founding, and both were therefore regarded as pioneers or veterans. In this pioneering and revolutionary society, "veteraneity" affords its bearer much prestige. There is good reason, then, to think that veterans will be politically secure, and to suppose that such members over the years will have forged sufficiently strong ties to protect at least their personal interests. Ketemyeh's father, however, was wanting in strength, as the case and its outcome demonstrate.

Most of Ketemyeh's father's career in the community had been given over to pig-breeding, but this was eliminated from Timem's economy in the early 1960s. In view of the emphasis placed on work in this collectivist community, and of the years the man had devoted to developing professional expertise, swineherding must have been a principal component of his social identity, and its elimination must have been a harsh blow for his career. Subsequently, he was shifted about, and to some extent he served as an economic "cork" (*pkack*), a pejorative term indicative of structural weakness. Moreover, the evidence suggests that he had always been at some disadvantage. Throughout his entire career in Timem (according to my data), he, no more than his son, had never once held an administrative post. Considering his long membership and the regular rotation of such posts, this is exceedingly anomalous.

In sum, it is clear that Ketemyeh was, structurally speaking, an invalid, and this must have conditioned the outcome of his case. But it is also clear that his weakness in the community's structure was odd, for it does not match with his advantageous origin as a senior son-of-the-kibbutz. The point is that there is nothing in Timem's social structure per se to explain how Ketemyeh got to be a structural invalid.

Stigma, Ostracism, and Expulsion

I have thus far talked of social relationships in Timem in terms of structural, categorical, and interpersonal principles. But social relationships suppose other principles which are logically prior to and different from those of social identity, namely, principles of personal identity. Clearly, social relationships require of their participants certain personal characteristics as well as certain social ones. Participants must be characterized as normal human beings, for typical relationships in the community are made for the normal person. Insofar as someone's personal identity is thought to deviate from the range of normalcy, his relationships become problematic, that is, social expectations are disturbed.

Criteria for normalcy differ from society to society, and abnormalcy is likely to admit of degrees. The characterization of Ketemyeh's fiancée as "not kibbutz material" meant that she did not meet with Timem's definition of normalcy. Although the remarks about her family, her divorce, her Iraqi origin, and illiteracy concerned her social identity, with the allusions to her ugliness and stupidity they combined to discredit her personal identity.

Ketemyeh and his father were also regarded as personally unfit. Long before I heard about his proposed marriage, Ketemyeh had been called to my attention. I was told that "the one with the limp" is retarded. I did not determine what the precise nature of his deficiency was supposed to be, but evidently his sexual behavior was taken as a sign of it. It was said that when he played chess with boys from Timem's high school (*mosad*) he harped on sex (to the delight of the boys). Another anecdote related that he once confronted a teen-age daughter-of-the-kibbutz with the painful opinion that her younger sister was prettier. Angered, the girl's father told him never to speak to her again. My informant added that Ketemyeh "is a boy in a man's body," and that every now and then his father locates a "misfit of a girl" from outside the kibbutz for him to marry. Only recently in fact his father had found another such girl—the Iraqi in this case.

I was told, too, that Ketemyeh has an extremely low I.Q. It was said that although he disturbs his neighbors (in what ways I was not told), he is tolerable as a bachelor, but that his children might not be normal, so as a parent he would not be wanted in the community. At other times I was told that Ketemyeh's "incessant talking is unbearable," that he had once been committed to a mental institution, and that "he is better now than he was in the past," the implication being that he had never been and was not now normal. I also learned that he had been dismissed from his job in the dairy (where he had spent a year before entering gardening) because he had been unable to fulfill his tasks adequately.

His inadequacies made him a target for jokes. For example, when some members were discussing the fact that the hair color of a child born to Ketemyeh's neighbors matched neither that of the child's mother nor of the father, it was said that Ketemyeh was perhaps the father. That is, the idea of Ketemyeh as an adulterer was ludicrous. He had long been the butt of humor, sometimes cruel. I was told by one of his age mates that when Ketemyeh had been in high school, the teacher (one known to have a reputation for sadism) often called on him, knowing that he could not answer questions and would only squirm under the pressure. No doubt, if more of Ketemyeh's biography had been known to me, my depiction of him in Timem as abnormal could be further exemplified.

Ketemyeh's father presents a similar picture. Discussing

Ketemyeh with various informants, it was said that his father "also has sexual troubles," is "also crazy," and is "not right mentally." I was told his father was subject to depression, for which he took strong medication. He was described as very "nervous" (*etzboni*), a favorite epithet for impugning instability. In this connection, it was said that Ketemyeh was a heavy burden to his father.

His father was talked of as an "idiot" (*tipesh*) and an "ass" (*chamor*). His behavior was interpreted in the light of these sobriquets. Once, during an open meeting of one of the Federation's higher administrative bodies, Ketemyeh's father took the podium. My Hebrew being inadequate then, I asked a member beside me what was being said. He replied that Ketemyeh's father always talks "nonsense" (*shtuyot*). I then asked if he were a member of the administrative body assembled there, and was told he was not, and that people were wondering why he had been permitted to speak at all. Another time, during a meeting of Timem's General Assembly, though no one had asked him to, Ketemyeh's father got up to adjust the lighting. As it was controlled by a number of switches, he only made it worse, which resulted in grumbling; eventually someone else had to correct it. Ketemyeh's father then closed a curtain in the hall, which elicited this remark from the meeting's chairman: "What have you done now?" Ketemyeh's father then rose to open the curtain. Such incidents serve to illustrate the general opinion that Ketemyeh's father was inept. In yet another meeting of the General Assembly, he rose and expressed his opinion on an issue on the floor, and another man, also described to me as an "idiot," spoke angrily and out of order against Ketemyeh's father's proposals. An argument ensued, and someone remarked to me facetiously, "It is going to come to blows." There was snickering in the hall. On another occasion, I was told that once, when some-one's dog got in his way, Ketemyeh's father hurled a stone at it. My informant commented, "The man is an idiot," and a second added, "He is an international idiot." Still another time, I was informed that on his sixtieth birthday, Ketemyeh's father had received a complimentary letter from a friend, and had been going around showing the letter, as if to say, "I am still somebody," but, my informant said, "He has always been a nobody." Finally, once when I was working with the dining-hall crew, Ketemyeh's father came to work. According to the work order (posted daily), he had been assigned elsewhere. When I asked the "head" what Ketemyeh's father was doing there, she replied, "He is assigned elsewhere, but what am I to do?" Her admission referred, no doubt, to the relative powerlessness of her position but also implied that he was be-yond helping.

Ketemyeh's father was also a target for jokes. As it was put, disapprovingly, by someone who had recently married into Timem, "Ketemyeh's father is simply a subject of laugh-ter." Once, as a work crew were on their way in from the orchards, it was exclaimed that the morning crew had managed to pick more apples. The head of the crew joked, "That is because Ketemyeh's father was on the afternoon crew." An-other time, at a small private gathering, the following story was related: "Once when working in the fields, Ketemyeh's father had started to defecate. When so-and-so—notorious for his practical jokes—saw this, he stopped Ketemyeh's father and told him a story about a man who had once been defeca-ting in the field when a 'green donkey' (a plant that jets liquid when stepped on) entered his anus and eventually came out through his mouth. After hearing this story, Ketemyeh's father never again defecated in the fields." In addition, his eating habits were disparaged. He was called a "slob," and I observed people avoiding sitting with him at the communal meals. Where people take all their meals together, and sit not according to preference but have to take the next seat available, the effect of unpleasant eating habits can be great.

Ketemyeh's father was aware of his stigmatization, as was revealed, while he was in the hospital, by an outsider who had received a letter from him. Not long after Ketemyeh's fiancée was refused admission, his father attempted suicide. This, it was said, "proved" that there was something not right with him mentally. After this attempt, Ketemyeh's father left the community.

The abnormality attributed to Ketemyeh and his father was also considered a family trait, I was informed that Ketemyeh's father came from a family of several siblings, a few of whom had taken their own lives, and that "although Ketemyeh's mother was an intelligent woman, his family is crazy." The way in which the whole family was characterized as abnormal was shown to me in a discussion about Ketemyeh's brother, who had left some years before. My informant said that his leaving was a wise decision, and that his sister, would also be wise to leave, for, "if people here do not respect Ketemyeh's parents, they will not respect their children either."

The identification of a whole family in terms of the traits of a few was common. Other families in Timem had been identified to me in terms of divorce, insanity, or suicide—which suggests that family serves as a means of personal characterization. Perhaps this is not surprising, considering that in the kibbutz, because the major part of a man's identity is meant to be collectively derived, the assertion of individuality is uniquely constrained. Since social identities are rather uniform in Timem, and furnish poor means for individualization, family, as the only major institution which does not derive from the collective, and so retains a significant autonomy, tends to be important for constructing personal identity.

The truth in the assertions of stigma about Ketemyeh, and his father and family, is not a matter of concern here. What counts is that such assertions were portraying, and thus constructing, the personal identities of those about whom they were made.

An assessment of the abnormality attributed to Ketemyeh and his father has significance for this case study. Failings are more odious to a community the more deeply they concern its fundamental principles. Ketemyeh's fiancée was considered unsuitable for membership on social grounds and because, according to the kibbutz, she was stupid and exceptionally ugly. These deficiencies must be measured against the community's ideological stress on social homogeneity, and organizational stress on face-to-face interaction. Hence, considering the extent to which everyday situations in a kibbutz are *social*, the stress on the girl's ugliness should not be taken lightly. The point is eloquently made by Goffman (1968:66–67):

Ugliness . . . has its initial and prime effect during social situations, threatening the pleasure we might otherwise take in the company of its possessor. We perceive, however, that his condition ought to have no effect on his competency in solitary tasks, although of course we may discriminate against him here simply because of the feelings we have about looking at him. Ugliness, then, is a stigma that is focused in social situations.

Or, take a member who is discredited because he is known to slack on the job. This is serious deviation from one of the kibbutz's fundamental values: work. Since the fruit of labor is theoretically equally distributed, slacking is logically exploitation, a social form against which the kibbutz was established. However, slacking is a matter of self-control, and therefore deviants can be held accountable, allowing the kibbutz to take corrective action, so rendering the offense less grave than it would otherwise be. Ketemyeh's failing, and his father's, struck at the core of the kibbutz's being—it was, so to speak, a representative failing.

Kibbutz ideology primarily resolves to eliminate "the contradiction between the individual and society." In brief, it argues as follows (Evens, 1970:2): Man is essentially free, as given in his capacity to create. But since in exercising this capacity, he is necessarily dependent on others, freedom entails cooperation. Where cooperation is weak or partial, as in liberalist society, the resulting organization acquires autonomy over and against the freedom of which it is a product, that is, a contradiction emerges between "creative man" and "social man," between the individual and society. But where cooperation is complete, as in collectivist society, the resulting organization is in keeping with its creator. For in the collective where all men participate directly and equally in the making of all decisions, no man makes a decision for another. In effect, individual decision and social decision are indistinguishable, and so, therefore, are individual and social autonomy.

However, should participation in such a society be compulsory, the resolution of the contradiction would be bogus: it would amount to the virtual extinction of "creative man" in favor of "social man," instead of a mutuality between them. Therefore, the establishment and persistence of such a society must be voluntary; the society must ever derive from man's creative capacity. This is "kibbutz voluntarism" (retzoniut). On grounds that collective life is both right and good, the individual is asked to embrace by virtue of both rational and moral choice. Clearly, if the individual freely consents to sacrifice his autonomy to that of society, and remains ever free to do so, he at once preserves his freedom and conforms to societal demand. Thus through a predential and ethical social contract, the opposition resolves into a perfect synthesis of "creative man" and "social man." One of Timem's ideologists, turning Plato's Myth of the Metals to his own ends, makes the point in this way (*The Book of Timem*, 1961): "The grace of giving [i.e., giving *up to community*, giving one*self*, volunteering] is the alchemy that turns a plain metal into a noble one, the name of which is Kibbutz; it is the catalyst whose very presence activates, amalgamates and unites."

As a corollary, the kibbutz's ethic of social control is educative and corrective rather than vindictive. In the words of the ideology (Amitai, 1966: 1–21): "The kibbutz has neither police nor courts to enforce the rules. Its chief means is public opinion . . . which educates the members of the kibbutz and keeps their kibbutz conscience awake. . . . Public opinion demands open discussion and criticism, the purpose of which is not to punish, but to correct."

Clearly, a system of this kind makes rigorous demands on the individual's rational and ethical capacities, his sense of responsibility. In the kibbutz, self-control is pervasive and marks even commonplace behavior. For example, I found that many members were embarrassed about taking to bed for minor illness, or were unwilling to admit that they were ill. Or again, females who cried out when giving birth were criticized. Exhortation to self-control had more comprehensive manifestations, as in the proscription on expressing ambition and on gossiping.

The kibbutz is critically predicated on the idea of a superior man, a man with an exemplary sense of responsibility—it aspires to, though concretely, Durkheim's "society of saints." Also, it is designed to produce such a man—hence the doctrine of *haben-adam hachadash*, the "new man."[5] No wonder that more than once I was told in Timem that the kibbutz contains "better people"[6] for, by its own plan, it cannot succeed without such people. Clearly, then, in this society the man who is known to deviate radically and essentially from this ideal would bear a profound stigma. Ketemyeh and his father were such men.

The assertations of Ketemyeh's retardation, internment in a mental institution, low I.Q., loquacity, poor work, and poor school performance signified a general incapacity for rational thought, and thus identified him as an inadequate kibbutznik. But perhaps more significant was his moral stigma, implied by the assertions of his sexual improprieties. From Genesis to Freud, Judaic-Christian thought has acknowledged thematically man's ability to keep in check his sexuality as condition and symbol of his moral nature and development. This ability is used as the measure of man against other animals, and against himself. Thus in Western society, children, because their sexuality, and self-control in general, are incompletely socialized, tend to be regarded as incomplete persons. That Ketemyeh was said to dwell on sex in his bantering with the high-school boys, served in the context of his sexuality, to identify him with boys—he was "a boy in a man's body."

[5] For an inside view see, for example, Leon (1964:L90ff.); for a penetrating sociological analysis pertaining to this doctrine, see Talmon (1972:ch.8).

[6] It is not only the kibbutzniks who make this claim. The French sociologist Georges Friedmann writes (1967:43): "On the whole, I believe, there is a remarkably high proportion of individuals of quality in Israel, and in the *kibbutzim* the proportion is especially high."

Obviously, such a misfit of a man would require a misfit of a girl as a mate. But his moral stigma went deeper than this. His immature sexuality implied metonymically a more general failing, namely, an incapacity to control his bodily self. Put differently, it meant that he lacked self-control, that he was not responsible. Consequently, he was representative of an ideal inversion of the ideal man. If possession of oneself is taken as a necessary condition of a human being, then the man who is lacking in this regard must be taken as less than human.[7] How much more must this be so where the ideal of self-control is, if not saintly, at least supererogatory.

Furthermore, because Ketemyeh's stigma was defined biologically, its social gravity was enlarged, as it was unchangeable. His improprieties were perfectly "defeasible,"[8] on grounds that stood beyond the kibbutz's system of educative justice. When he told a girl that she was less attractive than her sister, and her father forbade him to speak to her again, the father could have been expected to make public issue of it. To paraphrase Durkheim, in such a society even apparently minor faults can give powerful offense to public conscious-

[7] In an article about models of socialization, Robert MacKay writes (1973:27–28) that "children are incomplete—immature, irrational, incompetent, asocial, acultural, depending on whether you are a teacher, sociologist, anthropologist, or psychologist. Adults, on the other hand, are complete—mature, rational, competent social, and autonomous, unless they are 'acting-like-children.' Introductory texts in the social sciences suggest that without language and culture, newborn infants are not human, because language creates minds and selves. An implication is that children who are profoundly retarded or severely brain damaged are never human."

[8] As an extenuating circumstance, his particular incapacitation could defeat any claim against him. On "defeasibility," see Hart (1951) and McHugh (1970).

ness. But the father did not really have recourse to public sanction, for Ketemyeh was defined as unaccountable.

Ketemyeh's father was similarly stigmatized: referred to as an idiot and an ass, his behavior in public was laughted at. The joke about his not defecating in the fields for fear of anal invasion by a plant epitomized this contempt for his intellect. That he was deemed crazy, sexually disturbed, and nervous connoted moral instability. His reputation as a "slob" and the story of his stoning a dog had brutish associations, discrediting his humanity. A serious lack of self-restraint was conveyed by the tale of his boasting: he was a braggart. Where equality is meant to be uncompromising, blatant presenting of self is apt to be strongly disapproved. His coming to work where he was not expected was no doubt interpreted as irresponsible. The operation of Timem's economy depends on each man taking his place as assigned in the daily work order. When, confronted with the problem of Ketemyeh's father, the crew head expressed helplessness ("What am I to do?"), it suggested that he, like his son, was unaccountable. Indeed, the very act of coming to work there, though he was assigned elsewhere, must have seemed so anomalous as to call up the idea that he was beyond help. Finally, there is his attempt on his own life, which could be taken to indicate that he was infirm of mind, of self-control.

Ketemyeh and his father were, then, gravely stigmatized. This above all is why Ketemyeh's proposed marriage was an issue, and why the case for his wife to reside in the kibbutz was lost. The formal decision not to admit the girl was virtually one to expel Ketemyeh himself.

To be sure, there were other members of Timem who were often called "idiot," "ass," "braggart," "nervous," and so forth. But none were (to my knowledge) as gravely stigmatized. By virtue of their personal identities, Ketemyeh and his father stood on its head the kibbutz's intent to maintain a society of "superior rational and moral beings"—they were representative of the human conditions of failure of the kibbutz vision.

It is important to understand here the circumstances of managing stigma in a kibbutz. Any society is bound to have standard procedures for containing the disruptive effects of stigma (Goffman, 1968:58ff). For example, disruption can be curtailed by controlling and regulating information about, and interaction with, the stigmatized. In a kibbutz, owing to collectivism and communitarianism, such procedures are relatively limited. Most activity is public, and there is little that can be concealed from the membership at large. As members, Ketemyeh and his father had the right and the duty to participate in the daily public life of Timem. It follows that their habitual failure to take part in communal meals, discussions, ceremonies, and the like would have served only to accent their stigmatization, and would have added to the social tension contingent on it. Moreover, it was not possible to control closely information about them. Ketemyeh had spent all his life in Timem, and his father most of his, and their careers were well known, just as they would be in a family.

But the kibbutz does not altogether lack means of adjustment. By relegating them to certain positions and excluding them from others, Ketemyeh and his father were denied, ostensibly to everyday organizational ends, certain structural bases of power. This adjustment was most conspicuous in the crucial spheres of work and administration. In addition, when it was likely to be inconspicuous (or at least so defined), interpersonal avoidance was practiced. Thus Ketemyeh had little interaction with his neighbors, and could often be found taking his meal after most members had eaten and left the dining hall. Again, members could be observed at meal times subtly avoiding sitting at table with Ketemyeh's father (for example, on seeing that the next seat available was adjacent to him, a member, by redirecting himself—as if he had forgotten to look at it—to the bulletin board just outside the dining hall, could wait for another seat without ostensibly denying commensality.) In other words, it was their stigmatization that best explains why Ketemyeh and his father failed to secure firm footholds in Timem's social order.

Such unspoken ostracism is called by Goffman (1968:147f.) "phantom acceptance" and "phantom normalcy." Adjustment to this kind of treatment depends largely on the willingness of the stigmatized individual to refrain from entering social contexts in which the phantasm is difficult to maintain. However, I have just shown that the entirety of the kibbutz is such a context. Following Goffman (1968:146–147), a good or easeful adjustment allows "that normals will not have to admit to themselves how limited their tactfulness and tolerance is . . . and . . . that normals can remain relatively uncontaminated by intimate contact with the stigmatized, relatively unthreatened in their identity beliefs." Because the institutional framework of the kibbutz heavily safeguards the rights of members, adjustment there to stigma is likely to be, ironically, and however happy in other respects,[9] for both the stigma-

---

[9] Spiro's and Bettelheim's findings should not be ignored. Spiro (1965:50) said: "One case serves to illustrate the extent to which the kibbutz will provide for the needs of its children. A retarded child was sent for special training to the city, where it cost the kibbutz one thousand pounds a year to maintain him. When he returned to the kibbutz and required special tutoring, a valuable worker was taken from production to teach him." And Bettelheim (1969:279–280): "I was deeply impressed by the lengths the kibbutzniks go to in taking

tized individual and the community at large, taut, and relatively vulnerable once it is disturbed.

Up to the time of his proposal to marry, Ketemyeh had gotten by in Timem through such informal ostracism. But, evidently, his plan to establish a family constituted a breach of the conditions of adjustment. Although the original settlers altered the role of the family through the collectivization of functions belonging to it (mainly, economic cooperation and child-rearing), its form was unchanged: it remains today a biologically defined (cultural) unit, ideally comprising at least a husband and wife and their children.[10] The family is significant in the kibbutz as the only major institution which is not formally generated from the top down, so to speak. It thus enjoys a unique autonomy which affords members an important means of individuation and makes the family a very distinctive phenomenon. Furthermore, because it remains uniquely autonomous at the same time that the collective is discharging important functions "belonging to it," its mediating significance for the individual and society is, if anything,

---

care of the few children who are mentally retarded, brain damaged, etc. The whole kibbutz makes these children its concern . . . teachers make all necessary allowances and go out of their way to help them adjust to kibbutz life. I saw some of these children as grown-ups, and although one or the other of them was most difficult to live with and work with—obstinate, cantankerous, etc.—the kibbutz felt that they had to be accepted and special allowances made, not only because they were children of the kibbutz, but because one must make their parents (who are also kibbutzniks) feel their children are being well taken care of. I state this very forcefully, because it was most moving to see how wonderful they were about keeping such defectives within their society."

[10] See Spiro's addendum (1958) to his article on the kibbutz family, "Is the Family Universal"; cf. also Talmon's sociologically intensive studies of kibbutz family organization (1972).

increased: through the family, the two become genuine institutional extensions of each other. Children must enter the collective child-rearing system, where new kibbutzniks are shaped. As a result, links are created between the parents and other parents, and, more importantly, between the parents and the collective. Since both family and collective are sustained by children, these links give the family, and therefore the individual, the possibility of identifying with the collective permanently. Family has, then, a vital significance for both the kibbutz and the individual member.

Ketemyeh's intention to marry can now be seen to have been a major political move, a bid to stretch his phantom acceptance and normalcy to concrete dimensions. Though the formal events centered on the girl, Ketemyeh's stigmatization and the political thrust of his desire to bring in a spouse were the foci of the informal process. While the case was being decided. I was told by informants that "Ketemyeh's children might not be normal," that "he would not be wanted as a parent," and that "no parent would want his children in the same age group with their own." The question of Ketemyeh gaining entry to the child-rearing system was so important that (as two informants told me) the Secretary had, before the issue was to be raised in the General Assembly, consulted a physician on the advisability of Ketemyeh having children. The physician, I might add, thought it would do him good to marry and become a father.

Here, then, was reason for Ketemyeh's age mates to have failed to support him. Indeed, one member told me categorically that the veterans, "who are through having children," voted to bring the girl in on probation, whereas the young members voted against her. This member had not, however, attended the General Assembly meeting in which the decision was taken, and according to my evidence, the voting distribution was not so clear-cut. Nevertheless, the statement suggests that Ketemyeh's age peers were likely to have worked against him, if only by withholding their support. "If Ketemyeh and his wife proceed to have children," said an informant, "then the parents whose children would belong to the same age group would be unable to avoid relationships with the couple."

There is an aspect of the legal contract between Ketemyeh and the kibbutz that appears to be contradictory here. The contract was said to state that in the event of the death of one of the spouses, the surviving mate and the children that might result from the union would have the right to take up residence. Three points may be made about this. First, my information concerning the contract is uncertain. It may be that this right was merely rumor, or that although the right pertained to residence in Timem, it denied the possibility of membership. Second, if the right was in the contract, it may have been thought to present small risk, for, even before the decision was made to reject the girl, it had been rumored that she was sterile, and some months after the decision had been taken, I was told that it was certain. This rumor was probably based on the fact that she had no children by her previous marriage, though Israel's "Oriental" Jews place great value on having them. However, if the girl was thought to be sterile, it may then be asked why the fear of children was such a feature of the case. I suggest that the idea that the girl was sterile was regarded as mere rumor and so failed to allay the fears of the younger crowd. Indeed, some of the same persons who informed me of the rumor also believed that the fear was itself reason enough for rejecting the couple. In view of the underlying issue of extreme stigma, it is unlikely that this rumor by itself would have been selected as relevant to deciding the case; what must have counted was only the hearsay that pictured the girl as undesirable.[11] And third, if such a right was included, it must have strengthened the contract considerably in its underlying intent to guard the kibbutz, as I shall show, against legal recrimination.

Clearly, then, the decision to reject Ketemyeh's choice was also a decision to prevent Ketemyeh himself from securing a vital structural foothold and identifying himself integrally with the community. (The extent to which this was so may be measured against one of the decisions's consequences, namely, since Ketemyeh's only brother had already left, the decision totally dissociated the family from Timem's future.) Again, therefore, it was the stigma he bore that explains why his marriage became an issue and his case was lost.

If this analysis is correct, then the issue of the girl was more instrumental than substantive. However, it may well be asked why it was necessary to use the girl as a pretext. In other words, since he too was "not kibbutz material," why was Ketemyeh not shut out from the community long before? The answer rests in the kibbutz's ethos or characteristic spirit, and the kibbutz's relationship to its external society.

In terms of fundamental ideological premises, Timem had legitimate reasons for wanting to be rid of Ketemyeh. His mental weakness was, for their ideology of self-control and moral superiority, a moral one. But there are other fundamental precepts of the ideology which pertained to the case. First, the kibbutz is meant to appeal to and be applicable to all. It is a proletarian movement, admitting in theory no elitism but that of the masses, which, in a sense, is not elitism at

---

[11] On the nature of rumors as bases for collective decisions, and the part played by selective perception in this, see Shibutani's excellent study (1966).

all. The universalism of the kibbutz program is itself a claim to moral superiority, especially over the particularism of the capitalist paradigm, wherein only some have full social advantage. This principle of kibbutz socialism is connected to a second, egalitarianism. Kibbutz egalitarianism, although based on the presupposition of the rational and moral unity of mankind, has come to acknowledge that men everywhere exhibit individual differences, and in this partakes of Marxism. Amitai (1966:17) states that the kibbutz has as a final aim "a worldwide socialist society in which men will live according to the principle: 'From each according to his abilities; to each according to his needs.' "

It could be argued that Ketemyeh's case in no way contradicts Timem's espousal of these principles. For although kibbutz universalism and egalitarianism are meant to take into account the way in which men differ from one another, Ketemyeh had been discredited as a man. His failure to measure up to the ideology's standards of rational and moral judgment amounted precisely to his definition as less than a man.

The ideology per se seems ill-conceived to resolve, through any means other than expulsion, the kind of problem Ketemyeh presented. In fact, his case suggests that the ideology can scarcely acknowledge or comprehend such a problem. Kibbutz ideology offers a radically sociological outlook on man and his nature. It is focused on a definition of a man's ills and problems as social in nature and cause. Consequently, it resolves to correct these through social means by the radical reformation of society. However, Ketemyeh's disability, which was naturally based, did not admit of such correction.

Still, I think, Timem's members could not in such terms have rationalized outright expulsion of Ketemyeh, and it is evident they never considered such a move legitimate. The reason is that Timem's ethos comes to more than formal ideology. Kibbutz ideology is a systematic, self-reflexive set of ideas, meant to replace the traditional consciousness in which the founders of the kibbutz had been raised. But of course, the replacement has not been complete. Such an ideology is bound to leave unaffected, or affected as unplanned, much of what a man "knows" but need not, and often cannot, articulate—what he knows to be true and real *without any question whatsoever*, and may therefore act on *without giving it a second thought*. That in the kibbutz such taken-for-granted knowledge exceeds the limits of the ideology is apparent in the community's fluent, meaningful intercourse with its external society, the ideals of which are in many fundamental respects opposed to the kibbutz's. It is also evident in the kibbutz's internal social life. For example, a traditional attitude concerning the natural differences between men and women has, doubtless, operated in the kibbutz from its inception to contradict the ideology's position on the equality of the sexes.[12] In their everyday social life, Timem's members employ parameters other than ideologically derived ones as the measure of man. It was clear that in spite of the ideology's implicit definition of Ketemyeh as less than a man, the members saw him also as altogether human, and therefore, fully deserving of treatment according to the community's humanitarian principles.

Because it is more lived than expostulated, taken-for-granted knowledge can include in good order what are blatant contradictions in abstract thought. The two conflicting definitions of Ketemyeh's humanity were both relevant to his case. But as long as a final solution to the problem he presented en-

[12] I do not wish to imply that such an attitude is the only reason for the sexual division of labor in kibbutzim. Cf. Talmon (1965).

tailed outright expulsion, the more inclusive definition was given priority, leaving informal ostracism as the only adjustment possible. Laying claim to moral superiority, the kibbutz has need to show, to itself as well as to others, that it is better able than the outside world to care for the physically or mentally infirm (see n. 9). Although Ketemyeh and his father constituted an embarrassment to the kibbutz claim to being made up of "better men," to have ejected them would have meant not only embarrassment, but also a rejection of Timem's ideal of humanitarianism; it would have opened to question the ideology's concept of man and society, the community's expressed reason for existence. However, presented with the opportunity of resolving their problem passively, with less than conscious risk to their intensely humanitarian self-image, Timem's members allowed the harsh definition of Ketemyeh to take priority. The contingent problem involving the girl presented this opportunity. For Timem's members, then, the outright expulsion of Ketemyeh was unconscionable in the abstract, while the rejection of the girl was—in concrete, inarticulated experience—perfectly relevant to resolving the problem he presented.

But, even if Timem's members could have seen their way, by sophisticated argument, from ideology to legitimizing the expulsion of Ketemyeh, such a move would have been hazardous. For the kibbutz's performance is subject to two ethical evaluations, its own and that of the outside world. Since the kibbutz depends on Israel at large in a number of vital ways, it cannot afford to ignore its opinion. But the external society is defined as against the revolutionary kind of kibbutz, and therefore it is not bound to see things in kibbutz-ideological terms. There can be no doubt that the direct expulsion of Ketemyeh, however justifiable for kibbutz ideology, would have been judged and denounced as morally repugnant by the Israeli public. Indeed, in view of Israel's relative size and cohesiveness, if the news of such an expulsion ever reached the public, it would be the makings of a scandal. Here, then, is more reason why Timem's members would fail to make issue of Ketemyeh's stigmatization.

There remains to be explained the agreement to support the couple. Although the so-called undesirable character of the girl seemingly accounted for the case, and was so defined by Timem, the judgment of her character could not explain the community's offer of support and its decision to make the offer binding in law. Individuals who renounce membership are today given a small sum of money by the kibbutz in acknowledgment of their past contributions and in order to help them settle outside. This occurs despite the fact that the kibbutz feels no internal jural compulsion—according to the ideology, property must be collectively held and indivisible—to compensate these people. For example, at a meeting of Timem's Secretariat I learned that a son of Timem who had recently left was given such money as a contribution to his marriage on the outside. The amount was about $100.00, a sum which may be typical of such gifts.

If the decision to reject Ketemyeh's chosen was *only* that, then his leaving would have been *only* a voluntary matter, contingent on his marriage, in which case, the kibbutz would have felt obliged to provide him *only* with the typical small sum. But, instead, the kibbutz offered him his job and agreed to support him, his wife, and their possible children. This suggests that Timem's felt-obligation in the matter exceeded by far that which it exhibits in most other cases where people leave. I can see no other way to explain such an excess of care than by regarding the case as a virtual expulsion of Ketemyeh and his name.

Ketemyeh's parents had joined the kibbutz near its inception, and consequently were esteemed as veterans. They had contributed most of their lives to Timem, and the community must have felt a considerable obligation in their connection. Although such indebtedness is not directly prescribed by the ideology, it is an apparent feature of the kibbutz's social process. How much an individual can be said to contribute to the social whole is in fact an important consideration when it comes to doling out advantages and criticism in the community. Following this line of thought, the community's failure to discharge properly such an obligation might be expected to occasion guilt, a rankling awareness of fault—all the more so in a community expressly given to moral scrupulosity. In this regard, it is important to recall that in the kibbutz's rhetoric, Ketemyeh was the community's "son."[13] Timem's willingness to undertake the support of Ketemyeh and his wife was, in part, an acknowledgment, by way of paying a debt and allaying guilt, and the decision to reject the girl was also a decision to cast out their own son. That he was given the option of continuing in his job may be interpreted as help, since he might have found it difficult getting employment elsewhere, and also as a way for Timem to defray some of the costs it had undertaken on his behalf. Additionally, it must have served to take the edge off the underlying, expulsive intent of the decision.

The legal aspect falls into place here. I am not sure how the law of the State of Israel would cover a case of expulsion

---

[13] I owe this insight to Professor Melford Spiro.

in a kibbutz. But one case which occurred in Timem during the time I was there indicates that the legal system can be manipulated, with annoying consequences for the kibbutz, in the case of persons who have left the community under unhappy circumstances. Just before my arrival, a couple with grown children had renounced membership, because they felt they had not received their due place in the community. The details of their charge are not relevant here. Upon leaving Timem, they either filed or threatened to file suit in hope of receiving a financial settlement for what they viewed as their contribution. Negotiations between the representatives of the two parties took place, but no settlement resulted. During my stay, the dissatisfied couple attempted further negotiations, and the issue was raised in Timem's General Assembly. Although the Secretariat announced that Timem's legal representative had advised the community to disregard the suit, there was disagreement. Some even wished to effect a settlement. (Timem's Treasurer at the time was also brother to the departed woman, and he pressed for negotiations.) The case had still not been settled when I left. But, however things turned out, it indicates that the legal system of the State of Israel is not necessarily compatible with the law of the kibbutz. This is not surprising, considering that Israel's laws of civil liberties and civil rights are based largely on a liberalistic rather than collectivistic ethic.[14]

The dissatisfied couple was not expelled but left Timem

[14] "Israel generally enjoys the civil liberties and civil rights that are traditional in the Western democracies; and these are derived primarily from the principles of British common law . . . with a substantial degree of reliance on American judicial decisions . . . ," to cite one authority (Kraines, 1961:172). It is certainly of interest here that the kibbutzim have demanded special legal standing in Israel (Eisenstadt, 1967:174).

voluntarily, and it is reasonable to surmise that the legal consequences of expulsion would be more serious for the kibbutz. This would be true particularly of expulsion for reasons of personal inadequacy. It would appear that the contract was initiated by the kibbutz as a device to protect itself in the event that Ketemyeh, his father, or affines, were to start proceedings against it (especially the affines, who were said to be dishonest, and who must have been feared and suspected of attempting to take advantage of the kibbutz through Ketemyeh). The contract indicated that the kibbutz had done its best to discharge whatever obligations it might have been construed as having toward Ketemyeh and his family. It was meant to preclude, and failing this to undermine, possible contrary legal proceedings. It may have contained a clause to the effect that in the event of death, the surviving mate with his or her children had the right to take up residence in Timem, such a stipulation indicating sharply Timem's efforts to do the right thing.

In view of the possibility of such moral and legal repercussions, it may be wondered why Ketemyeh or his father did not themselves make their stigmatization an issue in Timem. It might have been to their advantage. Bringing to the surface these grounds of the decision could have thrown the entire matter into moral question, profoundly discrediting Ketemyeh's opposition. There are three points I can make in this regard. First, it is doubtful that Ketemyeh or his father could ever have succeeded in publicly defining the issue in terms of their stigmatization. The father did accuse the Secretariat of racism, but failed even there to carry the point. Their stigmatization was far too threatening to Timem's self-image to have admitted of treatment as a public issue. Second, I doubt that Ketemyeh was sharply aware of his lot, though I have no evidence on this point. During the events, he insisted—to the incredulity of at least one informant—on viewing the issue as centering simply on the girl. And third, Ketemyeh's father had been described to me, by several members, as an idealist, meaning that he was deeply committed to the kibbutz ethos. I had observed in meetings of the General Assembly that, on issues which were interpreted in terms of "those who support the ideology" and "those who wish to liberalize it," Ketemyeh's father invariably stood with the former. I learned later that just before he left Timem, he wrote a letter to a member of another kibbutz (the contents of which were subsequently revealed to some of Timem's members) complaining bitterly of his stigmatization in Timem, but at the same time taking pains to absolve the kibbutz of blame and defend its ethos. It is possible he was ambivalent about raising the ideologically explosive matter of his son's stigma.

I have argued throughout that the events involving the girl happened because of Ketemyeh's profound stigma, which was an embarrassment to the basic goals of the community. But as it stands, this explanation is insufficient, for it does not designate precisely the motivation. The functionalist psychology, that Timem, through the rational activities of its individual members, eliminated a threat to its existence is scarcely plausible. In no rational way was Ketemyeh a risk to the community—certainly what were considered his inadequacies as an individual could not have toppled the kibbutz as an everyday concern. His threat was essentially symbolic. Why, then, was the reaction so extreme?

I mentioned earlier that other members too were stigmatized. But virtually all of Timem's members must have, at one time and in one form or another, borne stigma. On the grounds that no individual in society is so perfectly endowed as always to measure up to expectations, nor always so well situated as to be able to conceal or excuse failure, Goffman (1968:152), piercing sociologically its deep significance, concludes that stigma is experienced by all members of society. Nowhere is this more dramatic, as Durkheim knew well, than in "a society of saints," where trifles are defined as criminal and perfect men judge their smallest failings with the utmost scrupulosity. Ketemyeh represented the inversion of a critical ideal, *but one to which no member could measure up*. As an extreme instance, he stood for the faultiness of Every-member, and therein for the *ultimate failure* of the kibbutz vision. His stigma went beyond any particular transgression: it was "representative": it stood for "stigma." Consequently, its threat was not intellectual but deeply emotional, striking at each member's self-identity. At the level of symbol rather than rhetoric, the emphasis of the proceedings on the notion that it was the community opposing Ketemyeh's cause may be understood in this light. The father's attempt to discredit the Secretariat's representation, by charging its head with bias, had to fail. It could only have resulted, as it did, in the creation of another representative body which, in the name of the whole (by the mood of the community), saw fit to move against Ketemyeh. In alienating Ketemyeh, the community was symbolically casting out its own essential faultiness, thus reanimating the kibbutz vision, renewing the conviction in its own meaningfulness. As a son of the kibbutz, a natural and real part of it, Ketemyeh was a more perfect vicar. The decision's deep motivation was vicarious atonement. In other words, the case describes a tacit and ritualistic form of sacrifice.

Finally—concerning the mode of analysis—the view of the normative elements of society as grandly manipulable is currently enjoying favor in the literature. In this connection, the

above analysis, if it is correct, should be moderating. The kibbutz is an exemplary normative system. Although "ideology"
is by no means uniformly defined and employed, there can be
no doubt that the kibbutz demonstrates the explicit and pure
theoretical type of ideology: it has a large measure of autonomy *vis-à-vis* other institutions and it generates its own institutional processes (cf. Berger and Luckmann, 1966:110ff.; and
Plamenatz, 1970:15ff). As an institutionalized and highly
sophisticated body of directive ideals, the kibbutz ideology is
an excellent example of a manipulable order—and, indeed, it is
typically being manipulated.

But to conclude that the kibbutz ideology is manipulable
is apt to be too simple an analysis. It presupposes that certain
far-reaching implications of the ideology were incorporated
by Timem's members, but at the level of lived rather than
reasoned consciousness. None of Timem's members stated outright that Ketemyeh had to go because he was "a rational and
moral inferior," and I do not believe that any could have ex-
plicated the case in such terms. Rather, they revealed this tacit
judgment of the ideology in synecdochic and elliptical utter-
ance—they spoke of Ketemyeh as an idiot and sexual defective, as a boy in a man's body, and so on. In other words, the
ideology was determinative, but its force did not lie in explicit
directiveness of specific behavior, but in its capacity to generate a kind of deeper knowledge that is directly actionable
because it is taken for granted (cf. Berger and Luckmann;
Garfinkel; and Schutz).

At every point of its unfolding, the case turned basically
on a discrepancy between the normative contingency of a
member's mental incapacity and the normative expectation
that all members be capable of rational and moral responsibil-

ity. The discrepancy was removed by acting on the *implication* of the ideology that such incapacitation logically defines a kind of antimember. This implicit definition was made decisively relevant through the contingent matter of the girl. Put in the abstract, the contradiction of the contingent and the normative was mediated by implicit knowledge, a third term which partakes phenomenologically of both the first and the second. By virtue of this transmutation of explicit value into implicit value and thus to action, it may be said that while it was being manipulated, the ideology was also manipulating. This substantiates the simple but profound insight (Berger and Luckmann, 1966:73), that "the primary control is given in the existence of an institution as such," or (Barkun, 1968:157) that "law does not so much prescribe as preempt" (taking "law" to stand here for any normative order). The analysis of Ketemyeh's case lends no support to normative determinism, but neither does it bear out interactionism.[15] Rather, it proceeds on the premise that social life presents a dialectic of process and design.

REFERENCES

Amitai, Mordechai. 1966. Together: Conversations about the Kibbutz. Tel Aviv: English Speaking Department, World Hashomer Hatzair.

Barkun, Michael. 1968. Law Without Sanctions. New Haven and London: Yale University Press.

[15] By "interactionism" I refer chiefly to certain social anthropological theories of rational choice. But, any theory which fails to give the normative dimension of society its due determining significance, including, e.g., some expositions of ethnomethodology (cf. Cicourel, 1970), fits here.

Berger, Peter L., and Thomas Luckmann. 1966. The Social Construction of Reality. London: Penguin Press.

Bettelheim, Bruno. 1969. The Children of the Dream. London: Thames & Hudson. Also: New York: Macmillan, 1969.

Cicourel, Aaron. 1970. Basic and Normative Rules in the Negotiation of Status and Role. *In* Hans Peter Dreitzel, ed. Recent Sociology, No. 2. New York: Macmillan.

Durkheim, Emile. 1938. The Rules of Sociological Method. Glencoe: The Free Press:

Eisenstadt, S. N. 1967. Israeli Society. London: Weidenfeld and Nicolson.

Evens, T. M. S. 1970. Ideology and Social Organization in an Israeli Collective. Ph.D. Thesis, University of Manchester, England.

Friedmann, Georges. 1967. The End of the Jewish People? London: Hutchinson & Co. Ltd.

Garfinkel, Harold. 1967. Studies in Ethnomethodology. Englewood Cliffs: Prentice Hall.

Goffman, Erving. 1956. Embarrassment and Social Organization. American Journal of Sociology, Vol. LXII.

——. 1968. Stigma. Middlesex, England: Pelican Books.

Hart, H. L. A. 1951. The Ascription of Responsibility and Rights. *In* Antony Flew, ed. Essays on Logic and Language. New York: Philosophical Library.

Kanovsky, Eliyahu. 1966. The Economy of the Israeli Kibbutz. Cambridge, Mass: Harvard University Press.

Kraines, Oscar. 1961. Government and Politics in Israel. Boston: Houghton Mifflin Company.

Leon, Dan. 1964. The Kibbutz. Tel Aviv: "Israel Horizons" in collaboration with World Hashomer Hatzair. Reprinted, London: Pergamon Press (1969).

MacKay, Robert. 1973. Conceptions of Children and Models of Socialization. *In* Hans Peter Dreitzel, ed. Recent Sociology, No. 5. New York: Macmillan.

McHugh, Peter. 1970. A Common-Sense Perception of Deviance. *In* Hans Peter Dreitzel, ed. Recent Sociology, No. 2. New York: Macmillan.

Plamenatz, John. 1970. Ideology. London: Pall Mall Press.

Schurmann, Franz. 1968. Ideology and Organization in Communist China. 2nd ed. Los Angeles: University of California Press.

Schutz, Alfred. 1970. Reflections on the Problem of Relevance. New Haven and London: Yale University Press.

Shibutani, Tamotsu. 1966. Improvised News: A Sociological Study of Rumor. Indianapolis: Bobbs-Merrill.

Spiro, Melford. 1958. Addendum to Is the Family Universal? In N. W. Bell and E. F. Vogel, eds. A Modern Introduction to the Family. Glencoe: The Free Press (1960).

——. 1965. Children of the Kibbutz. New York: Schocken.

Talmon, Yonina. 1965. Sex Role Differentiation in an Equalitarian Society. In T. E. Lasswell, J. H. Burma and S. H. Aronson, eds. Life in Society. Chicago: Scott, Foresman and Company.

——. 1972. Family and Community in the Kibbutz. Cambridge, Mass.: Harvard University Press.

[The Book of Timem]. 1961. The Book of Timem [in Hebrew]. Israel: Shomer Hatzair.

Epilogue: Uncertainties in Situations, Indeterminacies in Culture

SALLY FALK MOORE[1]

When discrepancies exist between ideology and social reality, what do people do? What happens when a community that idealizes communal harmony is faced with internal conflicts and contradictions? This book has discussed such questions. It is not that there is anything new about recognizing the existence of such inconsistencies. It is that attention to the ways in which they are resolved raises basic theoretical issues. One of these is the question, What is the relationship between ideology and action? In the past, a great deal of work in anthropology and sociology has focused on congruities between ideology and the organization of social life. Much current work is occupied with the lack of complete correspondence between the two, and the ways in which social processes

[1] The author wishes to acknowledge with thanks two opportunities she had to present this material publicly, once to the staff-student seminar at the University of Manchester and once to staff and students at University College, London. Both discussions were very helpful, as were conversations with Professors M. G. Smith, Max Gluckman, and David Lowenthal, my husband Professor Cresap Moore, and my colleagues Professors Barbara Myerhoff and Jay Abarbanel, to whom I first presented these ideas. I also wish to thank Professor Victor Turner for encouragement generously given and much appreciated.

unfold in the face of this lack of consistency. But obviously there are degrees and kinds of congruence and contradiction. This raises the question, What kind of analytic framework can be used to consider the congruities *and* the discrepancies between ideology and action in social situations? Processual analysis raises further questions. How is the time factor to be dealt with? How can the same analysis simultaneously handle continuity and change? How can situations which are small in scale be analyzed in such a way as to keep the larger cultural context in view? It is one of the objectives of this epilogue to propose a simple processual framework which may clarify the analysis of these problems. But first we will review some of the ways in which the relationships between ideology and social structure have been dealt with, and some of the implications of the term "process" as it has been used in anthropology.

Ideology and Social Structure: Congruent or Not?

Seeking or postulating congruence between ideology and social structure has been as attractive to utopian idealists and to social planners as it was to social scientists. Cultural and ideological materials have been as frequently treated as a blueprint for a new society (or some specific part of it) as they have been considered the reflection of an existing structure. Discrepancies have been explained away as the consequence of transition, of lag, of imperfections in planning and the like. Thus where congruence and consistency are the core of the analytic model, the absence of these characteristics in ethnographic fact can be treated not as an inadequacy of the model, but as a historical phase of the society being analyzed.

Quite a variety of conclusions have been generated by models based on congruence. Durkheim, for example, saw in religion a representation of society itself. When the Australian aborigines gathered together to whirl their bull-roarers, or to sing to make the totemic animals multiply, or to mourn the death of one of their number, they were, in Durkheim's eyes, *representing* and *reaffirming* the social group through ritual. Religion as he saw it, was both a focus of social cohesion and a symbolic representation of society (Durkheim, 1912; 1961 ed.). This is a mirror-image approach to ideology and structure. One reflects the other. Congruence is absolute.

Weber's view of the matter was more complex. He conceived of ideas and values as directly informing action, as a shaping force in the social order as well as a reflection of it. In his analysis it was the ideology of Protestantism combined with economic circumstances that made the bloom of capitalism possible (Weber, 1904–1905; 1958 ed.). Attached to each of his ideal types of political authority is a set of ideas that legitimates it—congruence again, but with more subtle connections (Weber, 1925; 1964 ed.). He specifically warns that "it is probably seldom if ever that a real phenomenon can be found which corresponds exactly to one of these ideally constructed pure types" (1925; 1964 ed.:110).

Like Durkheim, Radcliffe-Brown saw religion as a correlate of social order. While he said that beliefs and rituals should be studied "in action," he does not seem to have doubted for a moment that if one did so one would discover a correspondence with structure. He recognized that the parallelism was sometimes hard to trace. "In some societies," he said, "there is a direct and immediate relation between the religion and the social structure," and cites ancestor worship and Australian totemism as illustrations. But then he turns to other, more heterogeneous societies, in which there are a multiplicity of churches or sects or groups. In such heterogeneous societies,

Radcliffe-Brown says (rather mournfully, one feels), "the relation to religion to the total social structure is in many respects indirect and not always easy to trace" (Radcliffe-Brown, 1952:177). But he seems sure it is *there*.

On secular territory scholars have repeatedly pursued correspondence between kinship ideology and kinship organization, since Morgan explained types of kinship terminology as expressions of particular forms of marriage and groupings of kin (Morgan, 1877; 1963 ed.). Causal links have been sought between the actual organization of groups of persons on the ground and their ideas about kinship, such as the matrilineal and patrilineal principles, terminologies that classify kin and such. One general assumption Morgan made (which has been made since, notably by Murdock) is that at some *point in time*, at the apogee of development of a particular system, there is a logical parallelism between kinship ideology and kinship organization (Murdock, 1949). It is at this point of maximal logical congruence that ideas about descent and terms that classify relatives are presumed to have adapted completely to fit the pre-existing realities of marriage and local grouping. Morgan's way of dealing with discrepancies, with instances where there was no fit, was to assume that this was simply an indication of a transitional phase. His underlying postulate was that ideology was more durable than organization, hence that cultural expression would lag behind social reality. According to this view, new forms of social organization would arise first, and these would produce their corresponding systems of classification. Incongruities could be explained as the result of a period of overlap between old ideology and new organization. For Morgan, kinship terminology itself could be used as the medium for a social archeology. Primitive promiscuity, one of the specific historical reconstructions Morgan made on this basis, has been discarded happily. However, the notion that ideology can be more durable than the organization with which it was congruent remains a theme in anthropology.

Such, for example, is the framework of Murdock's *Social Structure* (1949), in which he postulates a sequence in which a stable kinship system is supposed to experience change. It starts with a modification of the "rule of residence" which eventually results in changes in the form of kin groups and, ultimately, in changes in terminology. Thus change is assumed to begin with alterations in "on-the-ground" organization, which subsequently produces changes in ideology. Incongruities between kinship ideology and organization are invariably explained by Murdock as examples of change, or intermediate phases. It is not our purpose here to discuss Murdock's results, nor for that matter Morgan's. Rather it is to point out that both of them see the ideological aspects of kinship as a reflection of organizational realities that preceded the ideology in time. Our purpose is to contrast this conception of sequence with the perspective of the social planner, the political ideologue, the club organizer, and the systems man. These are conscious organizers, people who plan organization. For them the ideology, the model, the plan and purpose, the structure, comes first, and the actual organization is assembled afterwards. These are two quite opposite developmental sequences, but both treat *congruence* between ideology and organization as a key concept, as the culmination toward which the process moves.

There is another approach, an instrumental approach, to the problem which also emphasizes congruence, but in quite a different way. Malinowski, Evans-Pritchard, and others have analyzed ideology as a legitimator of current political and economic activity, as a charter for the legal exercise of rights and authority. It was not the foresight of the ancestress of each Trobriand subclan which made her emerge at the very spot where her descendants would establish their village and gardens, but rather the hindsight of her supposed descendants, who justified their land claims by inventing her (Malinowski, 1935:341). Malinowski interpreted much of Trobriand myth and belief as an exotic legitimator for quite practical activities. The same can be said for the genealogical rationale of the Nuer political system (Evans-Pritchard, 1940).

In all of these interpretations, congruence is stressed. Whether ideology is seen as an expression of social cohesion, or as a symbolic expression of structure, whether it is seen as a design for a new structure or as a rationalization for control of power and property, the analysis is made in terms of fit. Yet on close and less selective inspection, it becomes evident that the fit of certain parts of ideology to organization is frequently on a very high level of generality. The Tiv and the Nuer share a segmentary-lineage ideology, but the composition of the local settlements of each is not at all the same. To read a constitution is not to understand how the political system works.

Today few anthropologists are exclusively occupied with consistency and congruence. Lévi-Strauss has put the question, "To what extent does the manner in which a society conceives its orders and their ordering correspond to the real situation?" (1958; 1963 ed.:312). Leach has said that, "When social structures are expressed in cultural form, the representation is imprecise," and the "inconsistencies in the logic of ritual expression" thus produced are necessary to the functioning of the social system (1954:4).

Turner has put the problem in processual and situational terms, "From the point of view of social dynamics a social system is not a harmonious configuration governed by mutually compatible and logically interrelated principles. It is rather a set of loosely integrated processes, with some patterned aspects, some persistencies of form, but controlled by discrepant principles of action expressed in rules of custom that are often situationally incompatible with one another" (1967:196).

Apart from some conspicuous rhetorical exaggerations of the pervasiveness of social structures and cultural patterns, few anthropologists, past or present, have been unaware that there generally are differences between ideal norms and real behavior. In recent decades what has happened in some quarters in anthropology is that there has been a shift of emphasis from the study of normative models to the study of specific situations and specific sequences of events. This shift in ethnographic subject matter has been accompanied by an intensified awareness, ignored at one's peril, that "ideological systems" as well as "social systems" are frequently full of inconsistencies, oppositions, contradictions, and tensions, that there is much individual and situational variation, and that cultural and social change is continuous, though it may take place at a more or less rapid rate and be more or less radical or pervasive. Even the classical British structural-functionalists, who are often accused by their critics of being unaware of all these circumstances of social life, were not by any means all unaware of them. They chose rather to ignore them in order to concentrate on the elements of order. If one reads the pronouncements of some of their representatives, one finds that they say quite explicitly that their models are "as-if" models, used as heuristic fictions, as selective constructs, that they are not offering a mirror for reality but seeking to understand the regularities in social life (Gluckman, 1968; Nadel, 1957:147, 154; Firth, 1964:12, 59).

But recently among the historically, politically, and situationally minded in British social anthropology as well as elsewhere, there has been discomfort with an exclusive reliance on structural-functional models, a discomfort that goes much deeper than worry over the matter of reification. A model that is artificially timeless and focuses exclusively on regularities and systematic consistencies is useful because it is selective; but being so selective it has severe limitations. The question repeatedly raised in the last two or three decades is, whether a focus on regularity and consistency should not be replaced by a focus on change, on process over time, and on paradox, conflict, inconsistency, contradiction, multiplicity, and manipulability in social life? (See Firth, 1964:59; Barth, 1966; Mitchell, 1964:v–xiv; Leach, 1962:133; Turner, 1957; Van Velsen, 1967.)

Murphy, who has written one of the most recent of these academic calls to arms, has named his book *The Dialectics of Social Life*. He says, "Social life is indeed a series of contradictions. . ." (1971:143). He calls on the anthropologist to practice "the dialectical exercise," which he asserts to be "simple in the extreme." The anthropologist should, according to Murphy (1971:117):

question everything that he sees and hears, examine phenomena fully and from every angle, seek and evaluate the contradiction of any proposition, and consider every category from the viewpoint of its noncontents as well as its positive attributes. It (the dialectical exercise) requires us to also look for paradox as much as complementarity, for opposition as much as accommodation. It portrays a universe of dissonance underlying apparent order and seeks deeper orders beyond the dissonance.

Essentially, his formula is to seek the opposite of everything that seems obvious, what is hidden behind everything that seems apparent, and what in turn is hidden behind that. Simple indeed! A major objective of the method he proposes is to uncover as much as possible the lack of congruence between conscious models of society and the way it actually works. He sees this lack of congruence as a central fact of social life, and as a central problem of scholarly epistemology.

Murphy's attitude is not unique, though he is somewhat eclectic in his interpretation of the place of these phenomena. His approach is very much in keeping with tendencies in the discipline. This is particularly so of two of his preoccupations: the concentration on "activity," that is, on process seen through particular events and situations, on people in action, and the stress on contradiction, inconsistency, and paradox. The cases and questions presented in the present volume embody these concerns. All involve specific situations in which contradictions, inconsistencies, and paradoxes in social life and ideology have had to be dealt with by people committed to a harmonious way of looking at themselves.

Are such contradictions and the lack of perfect fit between conscious models and social actions the dominant feature of social life? Murphy has argued, "It is the very incongruence of our conscious models, and guides for conduct to the phenomena of social life that makes that life possible" (1971:240). Certainly elements of incongruence are omnipresent, but so are elements of consistency, and elements of order. Order and repetition are not all illusion, nor all "mere" ideology, nor all fictive scholarly models, but are observable on a behavioral level, as well as in expressed ideas. There is frequently some underlying order even in the contraditions and paradoxes and in the way they affect social life, as Murphy himself suggests.

What Murphy calls "the dialectical exercise" is a good open-ended technique for scholarly exploration, but it is neither a classificatory nor an explanatory device. It is a lively reaction against the exclusive use of normative models, but since these are *passé* anyway the problem remains what to use instead, particularly as norms are themselves social facts. Models are temporarily useful heuristic devices, the purpose of which is to focus attention on particular features of social life and relationship. All societal and processual models are simplifications. But they help to sort out the complexity of reality into manageable problems.

How can one analyze such order and regularity as there is while fully taking into account the innumerable changes, gaps, and contradictions? I propose that one useful way is to look at social processes in terms of the interrelationship of three components: the processes of *regularization*, the processes of *situational adjustment*, and the factor of *indeterminacy*.[2] The conditions to which these terms allude are ubiquitous in social life. There seems to be a continuous struggle between the pressure toward establishing and/or maintaining order and regularity, and the underlying circumstance that counteractivities, discontinuities, variety, and complexity make social life inherently unsuited to total ordering. The strategies of individuals are seldom (if ever) consistently committed to reliance on rules and other regularities. For every occasion that a person thinks or says, "That cannot be done, it is against the rules, or violates the categories," there is another occasion when the same individual says, "Those rules or categories

[2] Lest there be any confusion, it should be made clear that "determinacy" is not being used here to refer to cause and effect. What is meant by "determinate" in this chapter is that which is culturally or socially regulated or regularized.

do not (or should not) apply to this situation. This is a special case."

Social life presents an almost endless variety of finely distinguishable situations and quite an array of grossly different ones. It contains arenas of continuous competition. It proceeds in the context of an ever-shifting set of persons, changing moments in time, altering situations, and partially improvised interactions. Established rules, customs, and symbolic frameworks exist, but they operate in the presence of areas of indeterminacy, or ambiguity, of uncertainty and manipulability. Order never fully takes over, nor could it. The cultural, contractual, and technical imperatives always leave gaps, require adjustments and interpretations to be applicable to particular situations, and are themselves full of ambiguities, inconsistencies, and often contradictions.

Every interpersonal encounter, every interaction may contain, on a microcosmic scale, some elements of this kind, some options, some range of alternatives. Even long-term relationships may "develop" over time. That is, they may be minutely renegotiated, or reaffirmed, or both, with every meeting. The observations of Goffmann and the detailed studies of the ethnomethodologists have brought into relief those nuances of interaction out of which there can emerge a mutual construction of social "reality." But the options are far from unlimited. To emphasize the potentialities within situations that depend on how the players play them out is an appropriate reaction against the most simplistic and archaic normative models. Yet it would be equally simplistic to yield to a vision of perpetual and total social amorphousness, unbounded innovation, and limitless reintepretation. An emphasis on the range of manipulability within microsituations does not do away with the fact that larger political and economic contexts exist, that common symbols, customary behaviors, role expectations, rules, categories, ideas and ideologies, rituals and formalities shared by the actors with a larger society are used in these interactions as the framework of mutual communication and action. These place real and sometimes merely apparent limits on what is negotiable. By definition this set of social contexts and cultural artifacts affects the form of the interaction, and usually profoundly affects the content and outcome as well. Every interaction contains within it elements of the regular and elements of the indeterminate, and both are "used" by individuals. This is true not only of small-scale face-to-face encounters. It can also be said of plans and actions on a large impersonal scale, as in administrative action and legislation.

The whole matter contains a paradox. Every explicit attempt to fix social relationships or social symbols is by implication a recognition that they are mutable. Yet at the same time such an attempt directly struggles against mutability, attempts to fix the moving thing, to make it hold. Part of the process of trying to fix social reality involves representing it as stable and immutable or at least controllable to this end, at least for a time. Rituals, rigid procedures, regular formalities, symbolic repetitions of all kinds, as well as explicit laws, principles, rules, symbols, and categories are cultural representations of fixed social reality, of continuity. They represent stability and continuity acted out and re-enacted: visible continuity. By dint of repetition they deny the passage of time, the nature of change, and the implicit extent of potential indeterminacy in social relations. They are all a part of what we have called the "processes of regularization." Whether rituals, laws, rules, customs, symbols, ideological models, and so on, are old and legitimated by tradition, or newly forged and legitimated by a revolutionary social source, they constitute the explicit cultural framework through which the attempt is made to fix social life, to keep it from slipping into the sea of indeterminacy.

Yet, despite all the attempts to crystallize the rules, there invariably remains a certain range of maneuver, of openness, of choice, of interpretation, of alteration, of tampering, of reversing, of transforming. This is more so for some people than for others, more true of some situations than others. In many circumstances the people involved exploit the rules and indeterminacies as it suits their immediate purposes, sometimes using one resource, sometimes the other within a single situation, emphasizing the fixity of norms for one purpose, exploiting openings, adjustments, reinterpretations and redefinitions for another. As in the *kibbutz* or the *moshav*, sometimes a whole community consciously organizes itself according to a set of explicit principles and rules. Such a community may enthusiastically turn to rule-making processes and orderly symbols as if thereby girding itself against the amorphous uncertainty of indeterminacy, trying to prescribe against it as against a contagion. Other collectivities embrace particular indeterminacies as part of their credo, valuing above all individuality and spontaneity and a certain absence of rules (for example, some antiplanning communes and the "happenings" of the Woodstock youth and the French students).

Turner has constructed a polarity of these collective ideologies. He considers them based on two fundamentally different kinds of *social relationship* which alternate and oppose each other in the course of history. He calls one "structure" and the other "communitas," characterizing structure as based on "norm-governed relationships between social personae," and *communitas* as founded on "free relationships between individuals" (1969:128, 132). Turner points out that over time, structured communities are subject to change, their rules are reinterpreted and redefined, they face new situations and unforeseen events and must make adjustments. In short, they may become less structured in terms of their original rules, principles, and plans. The opposite can be said of collectivities committed to an absence of structure, committed to indeterminacy. If they succeed in enduring over time, they often become more and more structured. Thus Turner sees society as the product of a dialectical process with successive phases of "structure" and "communitas" (1969:112, 203). He also recognizes their simultaneity. Turner's book *The Ritual Process* is subtitled, "Structure and Anti-Structure," like some sort of social matter and antimatter, in a dialectical relationship that produces the complex synthesis that is social life.

A number of the cases described in this book appear to fit the conditions of Turner's model, inviting analysis in these terms, for example see the comments of the editors. However, the analytic model proposed in this epilogue is only partly congruent with Turner's. For one thing, Turner is talking about two bases of *social relationship*, seeing them in opposition to each other (1969:131). He looks at the two modalities in many contexts: in ritual, in the social organization of lineage-based societies, and in the context of a wide range of antiestablishment social and religious movements. Throughout, Turner is concerned with complementary and contradictory complexes of social relationship and the ideas associated with them. But the complexes of "structured" and "antistructured" relationships and associated philosophies with which Turner is occupied can be seen as special cases of a much wider and more fragmented distribution of regulatory processes, situationally specific adjustments and indeterminacies in social life. The present model thus derives much from his basic concept of a dialectical relationship between structure and antistructure, but it is not limited to the special circumstances to which he has applied the structure–antistructure paradigm. There are much more general, in fact, omnipresent processes involved.

Process: Changes in Individual Situations and Changes in Culture

What is a process? Is a process history, a sequence in time of connected events leading to a particular result? Or is it concerned with repeated types of series? The term is variously used in ethnographies: (1) to describe universal contexts of social contact such as processes of competition, or of cooperation, and the like; (2) to describe series of events that recur again and again in certain institutional contexts, such as, political processes, economic processes, educational processes, and so on; and (3) to describe the kinds of circumstances that lead to certain results, such as the process of industrialization, the process of urbanization, the process of segmentation, the process of stratification, and so on. These are obviously different levels of specificity and range. All have in common the element of observations made over time. All involve movement in the fortunes and relationships of individuals. Some also imply social and cultural change. Thus on the microscale, all processes involve change because they involve alterations in the situations of the individuals involved. But they do not necessarily involve social and cultural change on the macroscale.

When Gluckman calls his book *The Judicial Process*, or Turner calls his *The Ritual Process*, they are indicating that, though they may analyze Barotse or Ndembu material, in the main their purpose is not narrowly ethnographic (Gluckman,

1955; Turner, 1969). They are identifying certain kinds of repeated unfoldings of events in an institutional context and in a regular sequence. The implication throughout is that similar types of unfolding series occur in other societies with different cultures. It is also clear that, as Gluckman and Turner conceive them, "the judicial process" and "the ritual process" may accommodate considerable change, though they operate within apparently stable formal frameworks.

In many theoretical writings "process" is contrasted with structure. Partly defined in terms of what it is, it is even more often characterized by what it is not. "Process" also is often the flag under which attacks are made on studies of "structure." A brief review of some of the dichotomies and discussions may provide a clearer picture of the current connotations of "process" in anthropology. Firth, for example, has long had his own way of dealing with process and its terminological predecessor "dynamic analysis" (see 1964:7–29 in which he reviews his position in relation to the work of others). His basic theoretical dichotomy is between "structure" and "organization." Organization is processual, "the working arrangements of society" (see 1964:45, republishing an essay of 1954). It encompasses all the decisions and choices that make up daily life, the nuances, the variations and the changes. "Social structure," in Firth's terminology, consists of continuities, the persistent and invariant in social life. "It will be clear," he says (1964:45–46):

that these concepts of social structure and social organization, though complementary, are not parallel. . . . Social organization . . . [is] . . . a point of view. . . . The two concepts cross-out each other. . . . The relation between form and process may be difficult to elucidate; it may be easier for us to make generalizations about form than process. But this does not absolve us from the necessity of studying process.

In 1955, a year after this was written, Nadel took issue with the notion that social structure was something different from process. He saw "structure" as an abstraction from repetitive events, and used "process" to refer to recurrent types of movement *within* social structures, "the mechanics of intake and circulation" in social roles and positions (published 1957:129–130). Nadel had two particular kinds of process in mind: (1) shifts of persons in roles and positions that are regularly relinquished, and (2) shifts of persons' positions resulting from "all conflict relationships," including, "all the forms of antagonism we normally call competition and rivalry" (1957:130).

Though he spoke in terms of social structure, Nadel emphasized that it was an abstraction, that it should not be reified. He quoted Firth with approval, saying, "The social structure viewed as something within the grasp of the ethnographer's account is a myth" (1967:153). Nadel had no illusion that structure implied total internal unity or coherence. "Our ordered arrangement," he said, "far from being a total one, must remain fragmentary. In a word, it seems impossible to speak of social structure in the singular" (1957:97). Nadel also acknowledged that there are necessarily questions about the relative durability and relative repetitiveness of various elements that are abstracted into the "ordered arrangement" called "structure." He fully recognized that there may be considerable areas of indeterminacy in a social system, for example: *indeterminate role relationships* not governed by established norms [in which options are "roughly unlimited" and the incidence of actual choices show a random scatter (1957:138)], and *zones of indeterminacy* in the "system" of social positions. (If one thinks of structure as an ordered arrangement of social positions and roles, then those that are disconnected, or not equivalent to others, cannot be fitted into a total order.) Nadel does not connect these kinds of indeterminacy with the term, "process," but simply shows by means of them that his definition of the structural model is only relatively and imperfectly coherent, determinate, and durable. As indicated earlier, process for Nadel is essentially "the mechanics of intake and circulation" of persons through a fixed set of social roles and positions (1957:129–130).

Ten years later Barth developed a model that used the basic form-process dichotomy that Firth had discussed. Barth added his own elaborations, and these have stimulated a great deal of creative work. Barth treats process as the opposite of structure, using process essentially as a means of understanding social change. He asks how social structures, or, as he calls them, "social forms" are generated. As core ethnographic datum, he proposes "transaction [as] a prototype for a processual model of interaction" (1966:5). His argument is that anthropologists should study transactions to identify the basic variables that produce particular social forms. These variables could then be used to construct "generative models," rather like Chomsky's "generative grammar." The generative models could be manipulated to produce a variety of social forms through the juggling of the variables. The model could be checked and tested by being compared with actual social systems. Barth complains, "We have been altogether too ready in social anthropology to produce special explanations for everything . . . ," and argues that his models are an attempt to generalize (1966:30). But a page later he acknowledges the difficulties attendant on making processual comparisons. "Admittedly," he says, "it is very difficult to maintain any great rigor in the comparisons. . . . Each new case introduced in the comparison compels one to introduce new factors as variables" (1966:31–32).

There is no need to deal here with the semantic and model-building niceties involved in whether one includes "process" within the framework of social structure or whether one treats it as something outside; whether like Firth and Nadel one treats "structure" as a myth, a useful one, or whether one treats "structure" as a distorting artificial construct, so static that it distracts from the study of dynamic processes. For present purposes these questions should be set aside. They involve an unnecessary either/or polemic. What is useful in these various writings is that taken together they suggest certain gross classifications of processual studies. They seem to divide roughly between the study of regular repetitive events having to do with the circulation of persons, power, goods, and information, and the study of events specifically having to do with processes of changing social and cultural regularities. In abbreviated outline:

A. *The Movement of Individuals through Roles and Positions*
   Repetitive or cyclic events that nevertheless imply shifts and changes of relations between or among particular persons
   - (a) temporarily occupied roles
   - (b) shifts and adjustments connected with conflict, competition, exchange, communication, and the exercise of power

B. *Changes of Norms and of Social/Cultural Regularities*
   Events that imply shifting and changing social/cultural frameworks and symbols; the generation of social forms
   - (a) from indeterminacy to determinacy or vice versa

      (i.e., the generation of social forms where they did not exist before, or the degeneration of social forms into indeterminacy)

  (b) the replacement of existing rules or forms with new rules or forms (i.e., the change from one kind of determinate arrangement to another)

What is immediately evident is that *A* and *B* are not and cannot be exclusive categories. The mechanisms of circulation and competition are continuously in operation, and they imply unending movement of individual circumstances. The persons they involve are interested persons, who often manipulate their situations and are not merely automatons passing through mandatory role shifts. These situations of relative individual movement may be *par excellence* the parts of social life into which questions of indeterminacy and change in social regularities are most immediately introduced. This is why "transactions," which Barth has emphasized, are in fact so often very revelatory. Through the observation of transactions, many of the detailed operations of the regular circulatory and redistributive mechanisms that change the lot of individuals may be understood, as well as the conditions of interaction that permit the introduction of or adjustment to certain kinds of change in the rules of the game. *Changes in the relative positions of individuals and changes in social regularities are connected though not coextensive phenomena. It is this connection which certain structural models have deliberately ignored.*

Structural models deliberately discount all that is not regular and all that is particular. Nadel says, "in progressively discounting the particular features of social situations . . . we prepare the way for the discovery of general characteristics and regularities, and hence of the lawfulness—such lawfulness as obtains—in the realm of social existence" (1957:154). "Regular" can be taken in at least two ways. It can refer simply to any repeated behavior, or it can refer to behavior that is dictated by culturally explicit rules. Lévi-Strauss has called models based on these two types of regularity "statistical models" and "mechanical models." They differ in that the former focuses on behavior and the latter on ideas; but they are similar in that both emphasize regularity, repetition, continuity, and consistency (1963:283–289).

The point has been reached in anthropology at which it may be more illuminating to look on repetition and regularization as processes in competition with other processes, rather than as dichotomizing absolutely between structure and process, or the static and the changing, or the consistent and the contradictory. This is certainly the implication of the work of the Manchester school in situational analysis, extended case study, and network analysis. It is the implication of Barth's transactional analysis, or current sociological studies that are heavily ethnographic, and the microsociology of Goffman and the ethnomethodologists. Needham has said, in another connection, "If our first task as social anthropologists is to discern order and make it intelligible, our no less urgent duty is to make sense of those practically universal usages and beliefs by which people create disorder, i.e., turn their classifications upside down or disintegrate them entirely" (Needham, 1963:x1).

Granted that structural models have serious limitations, some of the attacks on structural anthropology place unnecessary limits on the alternatives. Certain critics of structural models assume that "structural" is equivalent to "static" and that "processual" is equivalent to "changing." The problem with this view is that it excludes looking at the processes that produce continuities and repetitions, and focuses only on the processes that produce innovations.

In the cruder versions of this critique of structure in which process becomes too exclusively associated with change yet another blind spot is produced. If the categories of analysis treat *change* as in some sense the opposite of *regularity*, there is not sufficient place given to indeterminacy, to elements in situations which are neither regular nor changing, but are rather matters of open or multiple option. As soon as one inspects real situations supposedly governed by culturally determined rules, one discovers that even within such "regulated" situations there are invariably elements and levels of indeterminacy. This is very evident in legal studies. Change, as indicated earlier, can be a matter of actually changing the rules, that is, of explicitly replacing one regularity with another. Or change may be a much more subtle thing, a shift from regularity to indeterminacy, or from indeterminacy to regularity, or through the whole series of possibilities occurring in the way Barth (1966) has emphasized, through the cumulative effect of changing individual choice.

It is important to recognize that processes of regularization, processes having to do with rules and regularities, may be used to block change or to produce change. The fixing of rules and regularities are as much tools of revolutionaries as they are of reactionaries. It is disastrous to confuse the analysis of processes of regularization with the construction of static social models. The effect of this confusion is to discard from processual analysis some of the basic techniques of societal organization. Analogously, it is clear that not all transactional interaction produces social change. The negotiations of individuals within situations may themselves be so patterned or repetitive that they can perpetuate a social condition just as effectively as the calculated maintenance of an explicit set of rules. One can analyze the efforts of people to use in different ways and to different ends the regularities and the indeterminacies presented by their situations (or which they introduce into these situations). The presence or absence of social change as an eventual outcome is an independent question. An adequate processual study of change is inextricably bound up with the processual study of continuity and indeterminacy. An adequate study of what is negotiable in situations cannot be made without attention to what is not negotiable in the same situation.

An Analytic Framework

It was indicated earlier that one of the objectives of this epilogue is to propose a very simple framework to clarify the analysis of situations, a framework to take account of ideology and action, continuity and change, micro- and macroperspectives. The basic postulate proposed is that the underlying quality of social life should be considered to be one of theoretically absolute indeterminacy. To put it simply, in this model social life is presumed to be indeterminate except insofar as culture and organized or patterned social relationships make it determinate. The assumption is that it is useful to conceive an underlying, theoretically absolute cultural and social indeterminacy, which is only partially done away with by culture and organized social life, the patterned aspects of which are temporary, incomplete, and contain elements of inconsistency, ambiguity, discontinuity, contradiction, paradox, and conflict. It is therefore suggested that even within the social and cultural order there is a pervasive quality of partial indeterminacy. Even in matters where there are rules and customs socially and culturally generated, indeterminacy may be produced by the manipulation of existing internal contradictions, inconsistencies, and ambiguities within the universe of relatively determinate elements.

A further qualitative complication arises as soon as one considers the dimensions of symbol and form as opposed to content. Apparent determinacy, in the guise of regularities of classification, symbol, and of form, may veil fundamental instabilities and changes of content. The Constitution of the United States in a good example of historic continuity of a determinate form subjected to continuous reinterpretation of content. Seeming indeterminacy of form may, in turn, veil actual regularity of content. Another example: certain types of meetings and gatherings are carried on in an atmosphere of mandatory informality and apparent openness of options. Yet these amorphous procedures may obscure very firm underlying regularities of power and decision. Thus regularity and indeterminacy may be of form and symbol or of content (or most often of some mixture). This greatly complicates analysis. To recognize this is to recognize that an anthropology exclusively focused on clear regularities of form, symbol, and content, and their presumed congruence (whether "structural," "cultural," or "processual" in orientation) is leaving out fundamental dimensions. The negotiable part of many real situations lies not only in the imperfect fit between the symbolic or formal level and the level of content, but also in the multiplicity of alternatives and meaning within each, which may accommodate a range of manipulation, interpretation, and choice. Individuals or groups may exaggerate the degree of order or the quality of indeterminacy in their situations for myriad reasons.

An analysis based on the assumption that there are ele-

ments of indeterminacy, potential and present in most if not
all situations, makes it possible to interpret behavior in terms
of two kinds of processes: the first are of the kind in which
people try to control their situations by struggling against indeterminacy, by trying to fix social reality, to harden it, to
give it form and order and predictability. These are the kinds
of processes that produce "conscious models," that produce
rules and organizations and customs and symbols and rituals
and categories and seek to make them durable. This is done so
that the individuals involved can hold constant some of the
factors with which they must deal. A fixed framework of
rules or understandings has certain significant advantages. It
means that every instance and every interaction does not have
to be completely renegotiated in a totally open field of possibilities. It means that there is some stability and predictability
in people's affairs and that complex projects can be undertaken and suitable strategies planned on the basis of reasonable
expectations about the behavior of other persons and/or their
frames of reference. This would seem to be why people "constructing social reality," as the ethnomethodologists put it,
often try to make their constructs durable and binding on
others. We have called these attempts to crystallize and con-
cretize social reality, to make it determinate and firm, "processes of regularization." The second, the countervailing processes, are those by means of which people arrange their
immediate situations (and/or express their feelings and conceptions) by exploiting the indeterminacies in the situation,
or by generating such indeterminacies, or by reinterpreting or
redefining the rules or relationships. They use whatever areas
there are of inconsistency, contradiction, conflict, ambiguity,
or open areas that are normatively indeterminate to achieve
immediate situational ends. These strategies continuously re-

inject elements of indeterminacy into social negotiations, making active use of them and making absolute ordering the more impossible. These processes introduce or maintain the element of plasticity in social arrangements. We have called these "processes of situational adjustment."

In the effort to construct, insofar as possible, a social reality that suits their purposes, people may resort to both kinds of techniques, often in the very same situation. What this model provides is a way of looking at what is taking place in terms of its effects, not on individual fortunes alone, but on the solidifying or eroding or transforming or dissolving of cultural and social regularities. The effects selected out for attention by this model are the increase or decrease of the determinate and fixed in social relations and cultural expressions. The model takes it into account that determining and fixing are processes, not states that are ever permanently achieved. The fixed in social reality really means the continuously renewed. And it is clear from the model that the processes of situational adjustment are likely to make what start out as processes of renewal into processes of change.

What is also clear is that strategies used in situational adjustment—adopted, to be sure, in the context of immediate needs—if repeated sufficiently often, by sufficient numbers of people, may become part of the processes of regularization. Analogously, if new rules are made for every situation, the rules cease to be part of the processes of regularization and become elements of situational adjustment. Thus each of these processes contains within itself the possibility of becoming its schematic opposite.

This model, which provides an open-ended way of working with a great variety of materials, including the cases in this book that show a marked discrepancy between expressed ideals of community harmony and a more complex social reality, makes it possible to look at the long history of the theme of congruence between ideology and social life, and the newer tradition that emphasizes lack of fit between the one and the other, and see that both sociological attitudes may contain enough truth to be illuminating. There is no need to *replace* a past preoccupation with systematic regularity by substituting a present preoccupation with systematic contradiction. On the contrary, it is possible to harvest the insights of both. One can see the focus on systematic consistency as an analytic emphasis on the cultural products of the processes of regularization, and the concentration on discontinuity, contradiction and paradox as a focus on the cultural concomitants of processes of situational adjustment. Neither does justice to indeterminacy.

Ideology may be regarded as a product of what we have called the regularizing processes. Yet its instance-by-instance use permits the kind of reinterpretation, redefinition, and manipulation that is associated with processes of situational adjustment. Sometimes an ideology or part of it can be constructed precisely to cover the complex mess of social reality with an appearance of order, simplicity, harmony, and plan. But sometimes, and at other levels, the ideology of a society, or of some subpart of it, is not more of a harmonious whole than the on-the-ground realities. The fact is that when we speak of the ideology of a group of persons, or of a society or some part of it, we are speaking of it as a whole. But usually, in action, in particular situations, only pieces of ideology are invoked. Since ideology is used this way—piecemeal—inconsistencies are not necessarily apparent, as they might be when put together in an analysis.

It is this imprecision that gives plausible ethnographic support to almost all the various theoretical positions described earlier, even though the positions seem contradictory. The explanatory puzzle that remains tantalizing is that in some instances cultural representations of social relationships seem to be much more closely reflective of social reality than in others. There sometimes appears to be a remarkable degree of fit between ideology, or symbolic system, or organizational plan and on-the-ground realities. At other times and places, or in other parts of the sociocultural system, the fit is very poor. This chapter has tried to propose an analytic framework that could account for such a range of circumstances. If the assumption is made that in some underlying and basic sense social reality is fluid and indeterminate, and that it is transformed into something more fixed through regularizing processes, yet can never entirely or completely lose all of its indeterminacy, a great range of variability can be accounted for. Regularizing processes can be analyzed as they are tempered by processes of situational adjustment and both may be shown to be operating in a partially indeterminate social medium. All of these elements can be analyzed in terms of symbolic representations as well as on the level of social relationship.

This is a framework usable in the analysis of particular situations and their detailed denouement, and equally usable in the analysis of larger-scale phenomena such as institutional systems. It is perhaps worth reiterating that this is not a matter of analyzing the forces of systemic maintenance as they are unsettled by forces of change. Whether the processes are unchanging or changing is not the dichotomy proposed. Processes of regularization and processes of situational adjustment may each have the effect of stabilizing *or* changing an existing social situation or order. What is being proposed is that the complex relationship between social life and its cultural representation may be easier to handle analytically if the interlocking of processes of regularization, processes of situational adjustment, and the factor of indeterminacy are taken into account.

REFERENCES

Barth, Fredrik. 1966. Models of Social Organization. Royal Anthropological Institute, Occasional Paper No. 23, London.

Durkheim, Emile. 1912. The Elementary Forms of the Religious Life. Translated by Joseph Ward Swain, London, 1915. Republished, New York: Collier Books (1961).

Evans-Pritchard, E. E. 1940. The Nuer. Oxford: Oxford University Press.

Firth, Raymond. 1964. Essays on Social Organization and Values. London: The Athlone Press, University of London.

Gluckman, Max. 1955. The Judicial Process Among the Barotse. Manchester: Manchester University Press.

——. 1968. The Utility of the Equilibrium Model in the Study of Social Change. American Anthropologist 70:219-237.

Leach, Edmund. 1954. Political Systems of Highland Burma. London: G. Bell and Sons.

——. 1962. On Certain Unconsidered Aspects of Double Descent Systems. Man lxii.

Lévi-Strauss, Claude. 1958. Structural Anthropology. Translated by Claire Jacobsen and Brooke G. Schoepf. Reprinted, New York: Basic Books (1963).

Malinowski, Bronislaw. 1935. Coral Gardens and Their Magic. London: George Allen and Unwin.

Mitchell, Clyde. 1964. Foreword to the Politics of Kinship by J. van Velsen. Manchester: Manchester University Press. Pp. 51–107.

Morgan, Lewis Henry. 1877. Ancient Society. Republished, New York: The World Publishing Company, Meridian Books (1963).

Murdock, George P. 1949. Social Structure. New York: Macmillan.

Murphy, Robert F. 1971. The Dialectics of Social Life. New York: Basic Books.

Nadel, S. F. 1957. The Theory of Social Structure. London: Cohen and West.

Needham, Rodney. 1963. Introduction to Primitive Classification by E. Durkheim and M. Mauss. Chicago: University of Chicago Press. Pp. vii–xlviii.

Radcliffe-Brown, A. R. 1952. Structure and Function in Primitive Society. London: Cohen and West.

Turner, Victor W. 1957. Schism and Continuity in an African Society. Manchester: Manchester University Press.

——. 1967. Aspects of Saora Ritual and Shamanism: An Approach to the Data of Ritual. In A. L. Epstein, ed. The Craft of Social Anthropology. London: Tavistock. Pp. 181–204.

——. 1969. The Ritual Process: Structure and Anti-Structure. Chicago: Aldine.

Van Velsen, J. 1967. The Extended-Case Method and Situational Analysis. In A. L. Epstein, ed. The Craft of Social Anthropology. London: Tavistock. Pp. 129–149.

Weber, Max. 1925. The Theory of Social and Economic Organization. Translated by A. M. Henderson and Talcott Parsons, Oxford University Press, 1947. Republished, New York: Free Press (1964).

——. 1904–1905. The Protestant Ethic and the Spirit of Capitalism. Translated by Talcott Parsons. Reprinted, New York: Scribner (1958).

Index